AMERICA'S #1 ADVERSARY

And What We Must Do About It — Now!

by

John M. Poindexter

Robert C. McFarlane

Richard B. Levine

FIDELIS
PUBLISHING

FIDELIS PUBLISHING
ISBN: 978-1-7354285-4-3
ISBN (eBook): 978-1-7354285-5-0

AMERICA'S #1 ADVERSARY:
AND WHAT WE MUST DO ABOUT IT—NOW!
© 2020 by Richard B Levine LLC
All Rights Reserved

Cover Design by Diana Lawrence

The authors are pleased to note with gratitude, portions of this book have also appeared in *The National Interest* and *The Federalist*.

Fidelis Publishing, LLC
Sterling, VA • Nashville, TN
fidelispublishing.com

Manufactured in the United States of America

10 9 8 7 6 5 4 3 2 1

CONTENTS

ABOUT THE AUTHORS

John M. Poindexter, a graduate of the U.S. Naval Academy and the California Institute of Technology, is a nuclear physicist and a former Assistant to the President for National Security Affairs.

Robert C. McFarlane, a graduate of the U.S. Naval Academy, the Geneva Graduate Institute, and the National Defense University, is chairman of an international energy company and a former Assistant to the President for National Security Affairs.

Richard B. Levine, a graduate of the Johns Hopkins University and the Harvard Business School, is a former Deputy Assistant Secretary of the Navy for Technology Transfer and Security Assistance and a former NSC Staff Director for Policy Development.

FOREWORD

LtCol Oliver L. North, USMC (Ret)

America is at a crossroads. Our very existence as a free nation, in control of our own destiny, is at grave risk due to the communist government of the People's Republic of China (PRC). Absolute power in the PRC is wielded by Xi Jinping, China's leader. Intent on creating a false equivalence with America's presidency, Xi Jinping prefers to be addressed as "President of China," a title he has held since March of 2013. Xi, however, has many ominous sources of power, which have become unlimited.

Among his many titles, he is General Secretary of the Central Committee of the Communist Party of China, and Chairman of the Central Military Commission; Xi attained both positions in November 2012. He is also Commander-in-Chief of China's military and combined forces as of April 2016, and Chairman of the Central Commission for Integrated Military and Civilian Development since January 2017. Such a combination of civilian and military authority in one man is daunting in an undemocratic state. The world is now experiencing what Xi will do with this unbridled might.

Xi Jinping is employing formidable levers of power against the Chinese people, the United States, and our democratic allies around the globe. The PRC's theft of intellectual property threatens our national security and that of our closest friends. Xi's willingness to allow tons of illicit, addictive drugs to be exported to other nations endangers millions. His false territorial claims over vast expanses of open seas and the erection of man-made islands, which are, in fact, military bastions, provide visual proof of his determination. Even more menacing are the PRC's overt and covert actions to thwart UN sanctions against Tehran. As in North Korea, Xi's ruthless geopolitical strategy all but ensures the ayatollahs in Iran will obtain nuclear weapons and the means to deliver them.

Credible evidence exists that the Communist Party in China was instrumental in the worldwide spread of COVID-19. Religious freedom in China is non-existent. Democracy in Hong Kong has been crushed. The economies in dozens of developing countries are threatened by Beijing's "Belt and Road Initiative."

Here at home, the PRC's campaign of disinformation encourages Marxists and anarchist vandals to rebel openly against the principles set out in our nation's seminal documents, the Declaration of Independence and the Constitution. With millions of our countrymen forced out of work by the COVID-19 pandemic, more than a dozen of our major cities have been torched and looted. And now, with a presidential election just weeks away, Xi Jinping and his politburo in Beijing are hoping U.S. opposition to the PRC's repression and aggression will soon fade away.

As the three authors of this book document, the pace of Beijing's campaign of domination has been accelerating. These three God-fearing friends helped President Ronald

Reagan win the Cold War against what he called an "Evil Empire"—the USSR. They bring fifteen decades of matchless experience to bear on the question: How must the United States respond to the existential threat to our country posed by Xi Jinping and the People's Republic of China?

If Xi's PRC succeeds, every place on our planet will be plunged into the abyss George Orwell warned us about in his masterpiece, *1984*. Our children deserve better than being forced to exist in a totalitarian world where Chinese-built computers, artificial intelligence, surveillance systems, and technology monitor their every move, the words they utter, and with whom they keep company. That's not freedom.

Seventy specific action recommendations made by the authors are here in *America's #1 Adversary: And What We Must Do About It—Now!* Carrying out this blueprint in the years ahead will protect our freedom, our nation, and ensure the twenty-first century is America's century.

There is but one caveat:

Implementing the plans and policies in this book and turning the tide against Xi Jinping's goal of global domination depends on what happens here in our country on November 3, 2020. The outcome of this year's U.S. elections will be a turning point in world history.

We are oft told what matters most to American voters is their sense of personal financial opportunity. But, this year, the very survival of the United States as a force for peace and good in the world will be in profound jeopardy if we choose wrongly.

In November, there is but one candidate for president of the United States up to the monumental task of protecting the American people and our way of life from the evil designs of Xi Jinping's godless PRC. The sovereignty, security, and economic well-being of our nation depends on *We the People* reelecting Donald Trump.

PREFACE

by Richard B. Levine

The People's Republic of China (PRC) has accumulated a record of terror, death, and mendacity unequaled by any of the world's nations. It does such things for one reason and for only one reason: to preserve the power the Communist Party of China wields over not only the people of China—who number more than 1.4 billion—but over the multitudes residing in other nations China intimidates or coerces. To understand this threat, we must not dwell on surfaces and false reflections. We must be courageous enough to peer into the depths.

Kleptocracy means "rule by thieves." The People's Republic of China is a kleptocracy. Whether it be the persecution of political prisoners, minorities, its own citizens, or the citizens of Hong Kong; whether it be its monumental theft of intellectual property from every developed nation, most especially, the United States; whether it be its reprehensible indifference to the most basic measures to contain the deadly COVID-19 virus it spawned, the Communist Party of China has shown itself to be a great force for evil. The

PRC's strategy is to thwart the aspirations and the basic human rights of anyone, for anyone who yearns to be free is perceived, by means of its distorted prism, as being the enemy of the powers of a state intent on unbridled power and domination.

What can be done to thwart this malevolent power? Commenting on fellow philosopher Nelson Goodman's conception of the proper bounds of inductive reasoning, John Rawls proffered the concept of reflective equilibrium—the space in which we restate, reconsider, and adjust our beliefs, such that they may be projected reasonably to describe parts of the future.[1]

The constellation of possible outcomes concerning ongoing and future developments and challenges inherent in America's relationship with China, as well as their economic, military, and societal implications, may be reduced by reflection on America's history and the principles that have made our country great. Thus, through the application of reflective equilibrium, may we discern what steps the United States and the world must take in confronting an ascendant China.

Such reassessment, and the calculated responses that will follow, are predicated on one thing: the reelection of Donald Trump as the president of the United States. Joseph Biden, has, over his career, and most particularly during the presidency of Barack Obama, proven himself to be the coauthor of America's submission to China's patently undemocratic objectives.

China knows that with a sop or bribe of millions, it buys billions or more. The corrupted know the corrupt. Many institutions, governments, and persons have been compromised by China's schemes. That the praying mantis kills and consumes its mate to derive sustenance seems unbelievable and incorrect, until it is witnessed time after time; it then becomes expected. So it is with China and with unethical and compromised politicians who believe they feed on what actually devours them.

Of all America's political leaders, what can be stated unequivocally is President Trump has not been compromised by China. For his resolute opposition to the Communist Party of China and for many other things, America's president is deserving of the nation's support. America's ability to contest China is empowered by two great accomplishments of the Trump administration.

The first is the solidification and the enhancement of U.S. military power, for without such power, a national security strategy to overmatch China is destitute. The second is our defeat of ISIS, the radical Islamic terrorist group purported to be a nation. Its defeat by President Trump's assembly of forces did more than just crush a brutal terrorist group the prior administration first discounted as a terrorist "JV team," only then to consider it a threat whose defeat would take many years.[2] The defeat of ISIS reestablished America's deterrent posture against threats both known and unknown, for the life-saving premise of deterrence, intrinsic to any sane national security strategy, was eroded to the point of feebleness by the Obama-Biden administration.

MILITARY POWER

The framework for countervailing actions to oppose the PRC's aims has already been erected by the Trump administration. America's military power is the guarantor of any applicable foreign policy and national security strategy. To reach its full potential, America's military power must be marshalled and channeled, not wasted on unnecessary or diversionary conflicts. This is the essence of the Trump doctrine.

Before Donald Trump's administration, the Pentagon's procurement process was replete with the cancellation of new weapons on the cusp of production. This resulted, since the beginning of this century, in dead-weight losses approaching $60 billion, which equates to hundreds of billions of dollars of planned and expected weapons and systems the U.S. military never fielded.

Examples of canceled programs include the XM2001 Crusader howitzer: $2 billion was spent before cancellation in 2002; the Crusader was to be superseded by the proposed XM1203 non-line-of-sight cannon; it, too, was canceled in 2009 by the Obama-Biden administration, after expenditures of at least $18 billion in development and termination costs, including the cancellation of its sister, FCS vehicles. The RAH-66 Comanche, begun in 1982, was terminated in 2004 after no operational helicopters were produced; program costs exceeded $6.9 billion,[3] plus a half-billion dollars in termination fees the government was obligated to pay the prime contractors. The Comanche was superseded by the development of the ARH-70 Arapaho, which, too, was not produced, despite the expenditure of millions. In all these new programs, not one operational unit was fielded.

Other important programs such as the stealth, air-dominance F-22 fighter were terminated by the Obama-Biden administration after very small, inefficient buys. In addition, 750 Raptors were originally planned to cost $26.2 billion; the program was canceled after 187 operational aircraft were built at a cost of over $67 billion.

The Zumwalt class of powerful, stealth destroyers was to have been a thirty-two-ship program;[4] this was reduced to a procurement of three vessels in 2009, thus requiring the development costs of $9.6 billion to be spread over just three ships. Total program costs, for the three ships, stand at $22.5 billion, though per-ship costs were estimated originally to be approximately $2.5 billion, given a full program buy. Joseph Biden was complicit in the evisceration of both these critical programs, which were designed to carry our Air Force and our Navy forward with dominant weapons through the middle of this century. However, our actual programmatic buys, due to the Obama-Biden administration, represent nothing so much as a parody of both prudent defense procurement and the husbanding of national resources and assets.

The C-130 transport, the CH-47 helicopter, the M109 howitzer, the KC-135 tanker, and the Minuteman missile all began their initial development in the 1950s; the designs for the B-52 bomber date to 1948. Each of these systems is expected to be in service for many more years, with some weapons expected to have service lives approaching ninety years or more. Each system thus represents great programmatic success, for the initial designs have been upgraded or rebuilt extensively over the course of many years.

Infinitely less successful are the programs that attempted to create replacements or supplements for these systems. Of the replacements, many were canceled outright without a single combat unit produced, after the expenditure of billions. This march of errors has ended with the Trump administration. The military budget of the United States has been increased substantially from the Obama-Biden defense allotments that, if continued, would have compromised our armed forces and, perhaps, have presaged our defeat on the battlefield.

In consideration of these facts, emphasis must be placed on the development of weapons whose designs are robust, long-lived, and capable of being easily upgraded, repurposed or rebuilt. Attention must be given to modernizing existing weapons systems that may be updated so they may continue to serve with great purpose. This is exactly what the Trump administration is doing. President Trump has ordered a fundamentally new version of the F-15 fighter/attack aircraft, a plane never defeated in air-to-air combat and which scored its first victory in 1979.

This aircraft, the Boeing F-15EX, uses the plane's proven airframe, but modernizes it completely with cutting-edge technology and unsurpassed weapons carriage, to allow the plane to serve into the 2050s.[5] The venerable and, in certain ways, unequaled B-52 will receive another lease on life, for the bomber will get new engines derived from those in use commercially, to permit the plane to serve into the 2050s and beyond.[6] It will do so with a combat range unmatched by any aircraft ever built. In both these programs, the Trump administration has been guided by Ronald Reagan's example of the recommissioning of the four, Iowa-class battleships, which helped permit the United States to achieve unmatched naval supremacy, which sped the Soviet Union's implosion through exposing that nation's military inadequacies.

While never-ending increases to the U.S. military budget, in the face of massive national debt, are untenable, massive reductions in defense spending are not feasible given the range of threats our country faces. America's only sustainable option is to seek great changes and efficiencies in defense procurement and military spending so America's military may be put on a viable pathway. In this complex domain, the current administration is accomplishing effective, comprehensive, procurement reforms, based on tested business principles, to ensure new weapon systems are deployed rapidly and per-unit costs are kept low. Our present defense budget, under the Trump administration, is one our nation can afford; we cannot afford to reduce it.

At the same time it is making great use of existing platforms that may be modernized, the administration is committed to fielding weapon systems a generation beyond what was previously considered. Key weapons, several generations beyond those currently in use, may be fielded far faster than was considered possible by Washington's political class. This revolution is due to the administration's emphasis that defense procurement reform must be rooted in the best available business and contracting practices.

During the Civil War, the technology and the concept for a steam-powered tank were at hand. Such a weapon, mounting an early Gatling gun, would have been decisive for either army. In WWII, Germany could have deployed jet fighters by 1942, but did not: they thus lost air superiority in Europe. In the Iraq War, begun in 2003, the United States could have fielded nonlethal weapon systems such as microwave guns that could have substantially reduced armed engagements.

Throughout history, in battles where weapons or tactics were employed, which were a generation or more ahead of the adversary, immense advantages were conveyed to the innovating side. The Hoplite phalanx, Greek fire, the submarine, the tank, and the proximity fuse are obvious examples we must emulate conceptually. Too often, entrenched forces forestall the early adoption of decisive weapons. For example, in WWII, the advanced M-26 Pershing tank, mounting a 90 mm gun, was delayed for more than a year because the U.S. Army did not want to use its tanks to hunt German panzers: official doctrine held speciously that only U.S. tank destroyers, which were lightly armored, should hunt Axis tanks as a primary objective.

New, war-winning weapon systems, therefore, are now being pursued with vigor under the Trump presidency. The B-21 stealth bomber;[7] the F-35 stealth tri-service fighter;[8] the Gerald R. Ford-class aircraft carriers;[9] the FFG(X), guided-missile frigate,[10] which will provide state-of-the-art area air defense while achieving programmatic savings by being based on a proven ship hull; and a full spectrum of advanced Army and Marine Corps weapons and systems will permit the United States to retain the mantle of military preeminence into the foreseeable future.

Groundbreaking technology is of military value only if it is deployed at some ordained, future time. This is where America has fallen under past administrations. The only exception to this principle is the use of technological development as a force in being—which is a derivative of the concept of a fleet in being—in which warships could coerce a potential adversary, though they would remain in port.

A force in this sense may be defined as that which exerts a conspicuous influence, through its conception, its promulgation, or its existence, but not its use. An example of this is President Reagan's Strategic Defense Initiative, which caused the Soviet Union to doubt the continued utility of its massive ICBM and SLBM forces as measures of national power. This doubt, instigated by the Strategic Defense Initiative, helped speed the demise of the Soviet empire.

More recently, had it not been scrapped by the Obama-Biden administration, the Boeing YAL-1 Airborne Laser might have been useful as a force in being against the North Korean or the Iranian ballistic missile threat.[11] This, however, was not to be. The Obama-Biden administration cut funding for this critical program in 2010; the program was canceled outright in 2011, with this unequaled aircraft making its last flight that year.

What must be done? President Trump's national security blueprint must continue, for it will serve to remove structural and bureaucratic impediments to efficient, comprehensive procurement reforms, based on service-tested business principles, to ensure new weapon systems are deployed rapidly and per-unit costs are kept low.

During the next four years, efficient, multi-year program management and funding, a comprehensive streamlining of the DOD bureaucracy, with a concomitant reduction in the civilian work force, as well as structural changes to the National Security Council (NSC) and DOD, to include their relationships to the intelligence agencies, may only be achieved if America stays the course. Such a sensible defense strategy would be destroyed if a Biden administration came to power. American military strength and our nation's capacity to field war-winning weapons in the future would be gutted. The United States military, unrivaled today, would rapidly become a second-rate military power under the leadership of a progressive president who will prioritize political correctness, in all its forms, within our military over force readiness and America's recently imbued ability to exert force dominance over any battlespace.

Greater sagacity in our choice of conflicts and causes must also be part of our new strategy; this is what the Trump administration has so deliberately emphasized. It is imperative realistic appraisals be promulgated of both Russia's and China's military capabilities and intentions.

Although the USSR, throughout much of the Cold War, had the second largest economy on the planet and regularly devoted a percentage share of its economic output to its military that was two or more times greater than did the United States, Russia now ranks eleventh behind Canada in GDP amongst the nations. A nuclear confrontation between the United States and Russia, each possessing vast arsenals of strategic weapons, is unthinkable and would have unimaginable consequences. To militate against such an awesome risk, political and technological measures to promote stability, must be continued between the two nations despite the adversarial positions Russia holds.

Unfortunately, prominent Democrats have placed the garnering of political points, no matter how untrue, above the national security objectives of the United States. The creation of the absurd Russian-collusion narrative by senior members of the Obama-Biden administration is a supreme example of this treacherous gaslighting of the American people.

China, militarily, seeks to solidify its position as the dominant military power among the nations of Asia; its ambitious gambit in the South China Sea is emblematic of this intent. Though America has been the dominant military power in Asia since WWII, America's intent and its strategy have always been global in nature, bending action to comport with our worldwide objectives.

China's military intentions in Asia at one time were constrained, thus, reducing the possibility of direct military confrontation between the two superpowers. This is no longer the case. In Asia and elsewhere across the globe, China is using infrastructure building and trade as non-military levers. According to the World Bank, China's "Belt and Road Initiative (BRI) is an ambitious effort to improve regional cooperation and connectivity on a trans-continental scale."[12] Thus, America's arena of contest with China is dominated by nonmilitary fronts. Any military conflict between the two nations would be deeply injurious to both and would surely plunge the world into a deep global recession or depression. Therefore, military deconfliction with the PRC must be pursued by the United States, even as we contest this state in all other categories of national power.

THE DEFEAT OF ISIS

In March 2016, while visiting a military base in Jordan, Vice President Biden told U.S. forces ISIS was "on its heels," but admitted defeating it would require time. He stated ISIS posed "no existential threat" to America and the group's defeat would take "a long time."[13]

Vice President Biden's remarks were ludicrous and representative of his imposture, since that very same month, Secretary of State John Kerry stated, ISIS "kills Christians because they are Christians; Yazidis because they are Yazidis;

Shia because they are Shia."[14] The secretary added, the terrorist group's "worldview is based on eliminating those who do not subscribe to its perverse ideology."[15] For ISIS not only murdered religious groups within the borders of its caliphate, it mandated the murder of Christians, former Muslims, Jews, Hindus, and others throughout the world. Vice President Biden did not consider this threat to be a dagger aimed at America's heart; his secretary of state disagreed.

Not content with burying his callous mistake of four years ago, the former vice president has decided to rewrite history, for on January 14, 2020, Joseph Biden stated, "I was part of the coalition that put together 68 counties to deal with stateless terror as well as failed states. Not us alone, 68 other countries, that's how we were able to defeat and end the caliphate, ISIS."[16]

One can only deduce the former vice president is either brazenly lying about this grave matter or is in leave of his senses or both. His past and present statements concerning ISIS cannot be squared.

For the record, the Salafi, jihadist Islamic State of Iraq and Syria (ISIS) was destroyed by the Trump administration: just days after his inauguration, President Trump issued National Security Presidential Memorandum 3 on January 28, 2017, titled, "Plan to Defeat the Islamic State of Iraq and Syria."[17] In March 2019, the terrorist organization's final redoubt in Baghouz, Syria, was liberated.[18] In October 2019, Abu Bakr al-Baghdadi, the leader of ISIS, whose domain was once vast and crossed two countries, was killed by U.S. special operations forces on the order of President Trump.[19] This rapid campaign thus served notice to the rest of the world as to America's commitment to life and freedom.

President Trump has understood better than any politician of his day that to fight a group, a cause, and an ideology, it must be named with specificity. Ideological movements such as ISIS, a Salafi jihadist militant group—whose leader, according to a widely circulated biography prepared by ISIS, had a PhD in Islamic studies from the Islamic University of Baghdad[20]—can be defeated only incompletely by military forces alone, no matter their power. ISIS was a millenarianism, which is a religious sect that believes a transformative epoch is nigh, in which all things on earth will change. The spark giving this movement life must be extinguished; this is what President Trump has recognized.

For ISIS and its mirrors and simulacrums, such a comprehensive strategy consists of the following steps:

First, understand the theological and ideological underpinnings of the entity to be destroyed (including its eschatological focus, which is the establishment of the final phase of mankind: God's judgment of all humanity; the establishment of a Caliphate in Syria was central to this emphasis, due to their theological reasons).

Second, with overwhelming military force and with rules of engagement supportive of the mission, while taking reasonable steps to minimize civilian casualties, destroy the fighters, the structures, and the supporting infrastructure constituting the threat.

Third, mount a concerted campaign to discredit their foundational belief system. This is done by the exposition of logical, scientific, and religious errors inherent in their doctrine, leading to doubt on the part of adherents in the inerrancy of their malignant creed. This doubt must then be transformed into derision, in which adherents are portrayed, and come to be seen, and, indeed, come to see themselves, as absurd, for it is often the romantic notions of gallantry and martyrdom that draw many to the Islamic terrorist cause.

Fourth, support forces of moderation within Islam, including unyielding support to King Abdullah II of Jordan and to General Abdel Fattah al-Sisi of Egypt.

Fifth, nurture liberal Islamic movements, for Islamist alternatives present a threat to democracy.

Sixth, help create a multinational force, drawn from Muslim states and reinforced strongly by the United States, so it constitutes a force in being, to foreclose the future reestablishment of an ISIS-like entity in the Middle East.

On January 8, 2020, President Trump announced, "Today, I am going to ask NATO to become much more involved in the Middle East process."[21] Such an alliance structure may be built using available entities: the Islamic Military Alliance to Fight Terrorism (IMAFT), headquartered in Saudi Arabia,[22] whose membership stands at forty-one Muslim nations, is a useful step. The Cooperation Council for the Arab States of the Gulf (informally known as the GCC) may also serve as a foundation for such a coalition: the council consists of Bahrain, Kuwait, Oman, Qatar, Saudi Arabia, and the United Arab Emirates.

In the United States, the threats posed by Islamic terrorism or Islamism must be communicated directly. The transfer of monies from Saudi Arabia and Qatar to install Wahhabism in U.S. universities and think tanks through grants, scholarships, and endowed professorships must be severely restricted or, preferably, terminated (Wahhabism is a fundamentalist type of Sunni Islam, the official form of the religion sanctioned and practiced in Saudi Arabia). Foreign investments in U.S. media concerns demand scrutiny, for the American public deserves news and analyses devoid of an undisclosed patina.

ISRAEL AND IRAN

Of consummate importance to Donald Trump's strategy for the Middle East is America's alliance with Israel, all but torn apart by the Obama-Biden administration. President Trump has understood that if America and its European allies forge bonds of iron with Israel—Hamas, Hezbollah, and Iran will know they have no possibility of destroying this bastion of freedom. This will deflate such terrorists, bolstering the forces demanding peace. The chief antagonist to a peaceful resolution of the Israeli-Palestinian conflict is Iran.

The Joint Comprehensive Plan of Action, conceived by the Obama-Biden administration, Iran, and its supporters—better known as the Iran nuclear deal—was the flower of American weakness and aimlessness. President Trump realized this and, in May 2018, pulled the United States out of this deeply flawed agreement, while reinstituting the "the highest level of economic sanctions"[23] against this terrorist state.

By removing sanctions imposed by the United States and other nations and by transferring enormous sums of money directly to the Iranian regime in exchange for mild and largely unverifiable curbs on Iranian nuclear endeavors, the United States under the Obama-Biden regime created a high watermark for the price it was willing to pay for the most tepid reductions in a nation's nuclear-weapons capacity. This vastly complicated not only the opportunities to secure peace in the Middle East but undercut the potential for fruitful negotiations with the Democratic People's Republic of Korea on its nuclear weapons.

A ludicrous aspect of the Iran deal was its many sideshows, such as the transfer of $1.7 billion to Iran from America, ostensibly to recompense Iran with interest for its purchase of $400 million in U.S. weapons, which were never delivered. Indeed, it is almost tragicomical the United States paid $1.3 billion in interest to a Muslim state in which the charging of interest (usury) is illegal, for Article 595 of Iran's Islamic Punishment Law deems usury a crime.[24] Such payment constitutes the largest single sum provided directly by America to a state that explicitly supports terrorism.

Countervailing action by the United States was required to undo the damage wrought by the Joint Comprehensive Plan of Action; President Trump's decision to nullify America's acceptance of the deal and to impose economic sanctions, positions the United States to thwart Iranian ambitions to amass a deliverable arsenal of nuclear weapons. The nature and scope of the strategic offset to Iran will be one of the defining international-security conundrums of the next decade. Thus, the matter must be addressed now. The Trump administration's embrace of Israel as a strategic ally has served notice to Iran and to other terrorist or belligerent entities: America will not permit its alliances and interests to be destroyed.

Iran, understanding this new fortitude, seeks to form an alliance with China. The PRC and Russia risk severe sanctions by the Trump administration if either resume the provision of weapons to Iran after October 2020, when the United Nations arms embargo ends. This embargo is unlikely to be extended due to China's and Russia's presence on the U.N. Security Council. As permanent members of the U.N. Security Council, China and Russia were part of the 2015 nuclear accord with Iran.

The PRC began its nuclear cooperation with Iran in the 1980s; Iran opened its Isfahan nuclear research center with support from China, which provided research reactors. Isfahan is now Iran's largest nuclear research facility. In 1990, China and Iran signed an agreement on nuclear cooperation. Iran, in 1991, secretly received one metric ton of uranium hexafluoride from China.[25]

Once sanctions expire, Iran may be expected to pursue the purchase of advanced air-defense systems and fighter aircraft. It also might seek to procure new main battle tanks. Iran will attempt to make common cause with China and with Russia. A strategic offset agreement with the PRC is likely, trading a long-term supply of oil, at advantageous prices, for Chinese business-related technology and infrastructure as well as military assistance.

A major case of a Chinese national allegedly violating sanctions imposed on Iran is exemplified by the arrest of Meng Wanzhou, CFO of Huawei, by Canadian forces at the behest of the United States.[26] According to a Congressional Research Service report,

> The Trump Administration has subjected Chinese telecommunications firm Huawei Technologies Co., Ltd. to particular scrutiny. On May 16, 2019, the U.S. Department of Commerce added Huawei and 68 of its non-U.S. affiliates to the Bureau of Industry and Security's (BIS's) Entity List, generally requiring U.S. companies to apply for an export license for the sale or transfer of U.S. technology to those entities, with a "presumption of denial" for such applications. The BIS entity list decision cites "reasonable cause to believe Huawei has been involved in activities contrary to the national security or foreign policy interests of the United States," and notes Huawei's indictment in the U.S. District Court for the Eastern District of New York on charges of violating Iran sanctions.[27]

What are China's strategic motives with regard to Iran and are they part of a larger masterplan? China certainly seeks to secure a long-term supply of oil from Iran at advantageous terms. By leveraging its relationship with Iran, China may set this state, which is Shiite, against other concerned Sunni Middle Eastern countries. By so doing, China hopes to control, to a notable extent, the power dynamics for the entire region.

China built and opened its first overseas military base in 2017 in Djibouti,[28] a nation in the Horn of Africa. Djibouti's location by the Bab-el-Mandeb Strait, astride the southern approach to the Suez Canal, is highly strategic; the Red Sea is northwest and the Gulf of Aden and the Indian Ocean are southeast. While the U.S. and French military also operate out of Djibouti, Chinese encroachments in Bangladesh and in Sri Lanka create additional regional instabilities, which may serve Chinese interests as a powerbroker.

The geostrategic term "string of pearls" was first used in a 2005 report prepared for the Pentagon.[29] It describes the plan by China to build or to control bases of operation from southern China to the Middle East. In addition to its base in Djibouti, China appears to be readying a naval base at the port city of Gwadar, in Pakistan's Balochistan Province. This facility, which has been imaged by satellites, could substantially enhance China's presence in the Indian Ocean.

A dominant China could add still more bases from which to coerce. Thus, this communist state may seek to control directly, or through its surrogates, key choke points and sea lines of communication, including the Strait of Hormuz and the Suez.

Chinese scientists, engineers, managers, and universities will penetrate and coerce elites in the Middle East, as they have throughout the world. As Chinese technical, political, and military envelopment grows, American influence and our nation's basing rights, necessary for power projection, will be constrained.

China has also shown significant interest in developing its relations with Turkey. In 2015, a consortium, made up of three Chinese firms, bought 65 percent of Turkey's third largest container terminal for $940 million. Kumport Terminal, located on the European side of Istanbul is able to handle 2,100,000 TEU (twenty-foot equivalent units) in annual capacity and is a crucial interchange for China to the Black Sea and between Asia and Europe.

While tens of thousands of Uyghur Muslims have fled to Turkey for safety from China's communist regime, there have been increasing reports of Turkey's bowing to Chinese pressure and arresting Uyghurs, who live in that Islamic country. Some have evidently been deported from Turkey and may have fallen into the PRC's hands. If these allegations be proven, they demonstrate China's economic and coercive power, if wielded unmercifully, can exceed the force of a shared faith.

Complicating America's calculus in this region is the relationship between Iran and Turkey. These countries signed an energy agreement in which 9.5 billion cubic meters of natural gas will be supplied per year from Iran. Turkey's intentions in this domain were crystalized by the nation's contravention of America's wishes: according to an August 8, 2018 report by Reuters, "Turkey will continue to buy natural gas from Iran in line with its long-term supply contract . . . after U.S. President Donald Trump threatened that anyone trading with Iran will not do business with America."[30]

Turkey's President Recep Tayyip Erdoğan has upended his country's modern history as a secular state, which was stipulated by a 1928 amendment to the national constitution of 1924. Erdoğan's regime borders on being a dictatorship. His delusions of grandeur are gargantuan and have been manifested physically in the construction of what is by far the largest presidential palace in the world: at 3,200,000 square feet, it is fifty-eight times larger than the White House.

Though Turkey has been a member of NATO since 1952, Erdoğan has set a divergent course for his nation. He has bought Russia's S-400 surface-to-air missile system (SAM), which is not interoperable with the defense systems of other NATO states. Though Turkey was part of the F-35 stealth fighter consortium, the purchase of the Russian air-defense system placed the plane's superiority at risk. U.S. General Tod Wolters noted, "Anything that an S-400 can do that affords it the ability to better understand a capability like the F-35 is certainly not to the advantage of the coalition."[31]

Transfers of F-35s to Turkey were suspended by the Trump administration in response; the U.S. Air Force now plans to buy the planes Lockheed Martin built for that country, effectively removing Turkey from the program.

Turkey is moving away from NATO and the alliance's security objectives because of Erdoğan's matchless ambitions. Given these desires, what would Turkey most fear? The answer is a resurgent America demanding NATO's nations increase their defense contributions to the alliance. This was Donald Trump's promise; as president, he has spurred many NATO nations, including Germany and France, to commit to increased defense spending. A strong NATO, however, is not in Erdoğan's interests.

Ahead of a December 2017 Organization of Islamic Cooperation (OIC) summit, the Turkish newspaper *Yeni Şafak*, which is closely associated with Erdoğan's Justice and Development Party (AKP), called for the OIC to be part of a pan-Islamic army comprised of 5,000,000 soldiers, supported by a combined military budget of $175 billion.[32] This force, though implausible as presented, would be by far the largest standing army in the world. Erdoğan's revanchist regime, which seeks the reestablishment of an Ottoman Empire, which was destroyed by World War I, does view a pan-Islamic army, in some form, as an objective.

This dream is not an idle one. Turkey has established military bases within the last several years in Azerbaijan, Qatar, Somalia, and Syria. These are in addition to its long-established cantonment in Northern Cyprus and a presence in Iraq, which, on April 25, 2017, facilitated a Turkish attack on the town of Sinjar. Significantly, Vladimir Putin, Recep Tayyip Erdoğan, and Hassan Rouhani of Iran met in Ankara in early April 2018 to formulate Syria's future, which is indicative of a new comity, marked by reinforcing initiatives between these states.

America's current tension with Turkey has not arisen overnight, the stillborn 2016 coup d'état laid bare the U.S.-Turkey divide. Electricity was cut to America's air base at Incirlik by the Erdoğan regime; a no-fly order was issued for American aircraft. Indeed, the Pentagon confirmed at the time, "U.S. facilities at Incirlik are operating on internal power sources."[33] President Trump has confirmed the scope of contention. Turkey is now at a crossroads; it can either repair its relations with America and the other members of NATO, or it can cast its lot with China and Russia, make common cause with Iran, and by so doing become a pariah state.

In considering these relationships involving China, it is important to recollect how difficult it was for Egyptian president Anwar al-Sadat to dislodge the Soviet Union from Egypt. Sadat launched Egypt's Corrective Revolution in 1971, which decoupled Egypt from the Soviet Union in order to supplant the socialist ideology installed by Gamal Abdel Nasser, Sadat's predecessor; this reversal led ultimately to the breakup of the Arab Socialist Union party, which was founded by Nasser in 1962. Such courage, which would be required to displace a predatory China from within a client state, would be very difficult to summon today. Therefore, China must not be allowed to increase its footprint in a region so central to world peace and stability.

A multifactorial response by the United States is mandatory if we are to block China's ambitions. In doing so, we must also supply the weaponry needed to defend Arab nations from attack by Iran.

There are positive signs that such a strategy, if pursued, will be a success. Saudi Arabia's employment of its Patriot ABM system, to intercept flights of ballistic missiles launched by Iranian-backed Houthi insurgents, and the Kingdom's intent to acquire seven THAAD ABM batteries for $13.5 billion and to spend an additional \$6.65 billion on enhancements to their Patriot system must be factored into a comprehensive strategy to thwart both Iran and China in the region, for these ABM systems constitute a de facto strategic defense to oppose the Iranian ballistic missile force that may, in the future, be surmounted by nuclear weapons.

In contradistinction to China's and Russia's plans to co-opt elites within countries in the Middle East and in Africa, an opposing coalition comprised of America, Britain, India, and nations of the Commonwealth must fashion an alternative model of development to become a watershed. Ibn Rushd, the twelfth-century polymath, made outstanding contributions in physics, in mathematics, and in philosophy. It is he who should serve as an exemplar of the types of minds non-exploitative development may create. It may be hoped a new Arab cohort of Ibn Rushd's may battle today's extremists and Islamists, as he did against the fundamentalist Al-Ghazali. Thus, science can lead to the expansion of the collective mind through the instigation of rationalism.

Heretofore, the Middle East has attracted a low percentage of global, foreign, direct investment: there is little economic diversification. Substantial inequities exist between urban and rural populations, and looming, forecasted reductions in precipitation will be devastating if comprehensive measures are not now begun to husband all resources.

Immediate steps are thus required to diversify Middle Eastern economies by embracing new technologies promising efficiencies; thankfully, it seems the leaders of Saudi Arabia and the leaders of the other GCC states understand these needs. Therefore, American-led development may forestall Chinese hegemonic intentions.

"When the facts change, I change my mind. What do you do, sir?" Alternatively attributed to John Maynard Keynes, Paul Samuelson, or Sir Winston Churchill, this statement and question speaks to the mutability of knowledge. It is not an embarrassment to have thought development and wealth would transform the PRC; it is, however, a dereliction of our God-given reason to not realize, in the wake of the present pandemic and China's deplorable actions, the true nature of this communist regime.

CHAPTER ONE

U.S. NATIONAL STRATEGY POST-CORONAVIRUS

King Lear enjoined, "Come not between the dragon and his wrath," but this we must do to upend the fury emanating from the greatest foe America faces in the world today. The People's Republic of China (PRC), which is controlled by the communist party of that nation, represents a danger unlike any other to America and to our cherished way of life.

The declaration by Goethe, "None are more hopelessly enslaved than those who falsely believe they are free," concerns the fabricated semblance of freedom, which humbles humankind. After Tiananmen Square in 1989, Western elites misjudged the course charted by the PRC. Our leaders thought that after the fall of the Soviet Empire, the PRC's adaptation of capitalism would inevitably lead to a pluralistic form of government.

China, infused with American and other foreign capital and technology, was creating great wealth and with it, multimillionaires. Surely, this was capitalism, which would lead to democracy and to freedom for the Chinese people.

What was not understood was an alternative national model fusing party control and the eradication of internal opposition with an ostensibly capitalistic structure. The PRC, in its economic measures and in its ruthless suppression of dissent and targeted minorities, in fact, resembles the prewar form of the National Socialist German Workers' Party. Wilhelm Messerschmitt, the Krupp family, Hermann Schmitz of IG Farben, and Claude Dornier, among others, were inventors and industrialists who became extraordinarily wealthy in the 1930s due to Germany's rearmament and industrialization efforts. For China, the rigid communist system was poison. The socialist model of prewar Germany was different: what Germany accomplished, economically, scientifically, and militarily, if scaled up from a European country of moderate size and population to one the size and scope of China, could dominate the world. Despite the myriad of names China has coined for its economic reforms and plans, this is the essence of the model the PRC adopted after the fall of the USSR but masked to the outside world.

For the PRC to continue its march and still be a semblance of its original creation, pitiless political and ideological suppression, theft of intellectual property, harassment, and deceit would need to remain cloaked. Access to foreign capital was undergirded by the regime's insincere homages to freedom and to democratic principles. These flourishes concerning liberty were enough to seduce or to co-opt the elites in the countries of the world, giving China the sustenance required to build its repressive empire.

Indicative of our lassitude is the case of Liu Xiaobo, sentenced in 2009 to eleven years of imprisonment for writing parts of the Charter 08 manifesto, which demanded political freedoms within China. Liu's incarceration was not met by any meaningful action on the West's part to curtail China's access to foreign capital or technology. Liu received the 2010

Nobel Peace Prize but he remained in prison until his release in 2017, granted only after he was diagnosed with terminal liver cancer.[34]

The observation that fake magic is real and, conversely, real magic is fake, describes the difference between imagined expectation and truth. In the former case, we harbor the thought that the display, which we only observe partially, may be real, though we know it to be false. China's narrative concerning its adherence to democratic principles has supported the world's desire to accept the Communist Party of China's account of the genesis and the evolution of the Wuhan virus. This caustic mental haze has become rooted within our governmental, academic, and business leaders. We, as a society, appear willing to be led on a course presaging catastrophe. This blindness must end. If China's actions in the coronavirus catastrophe offer any window into this communist regime's deceit and its debasement of human life, it is that the threat the PRC represents is unique in American history.

Communism is responsible for the deaths of tens of millions of Chinese. To contend that aspects of China's government emulate the characteristics of a cursed regime is to rupture the world order. However, the people of Tibet cry out. The Muslims, Christians, and other men and women of faith in China cry out, and today, the citizens of Hong Kong wail, as do all those touched by the coronavirus. Do we not hear?

In its pursuit of unchecked power, the PRC resembles the ouroboros—a dragon striving to devour itself—for the sustenance this nation derives from the West and from capitalism feeds the Communist Party of China's quest to destroy that which it consumes. In all, the ouroboros represents both the beginning and the ending of time, which equates, most particularly, to the termination of the legacy of China's Century of Humiliation, which began with the Opium Wars and with China's submission to an assembly of Western powers, and later to Russia and to Japan, from 1839 to the beginning of the communist epoch in 1949.

The PRC's emergence and its recent actions thus bear relation to the concept of creative destruction as formulated by the Austrian-American economist Joseph Schumpeter (*Capitalism, Socialism and Democracy* [1942]). Creative destruction, though now applied to various capitalistic practices, was derived from Marxist thought. As the name implies, it argues that the destruction of what "was" is necessary to create the clean slate on which new creation may rest. This is China's path as charted by its communist party. By our nation's inaction, we have seemingly accepted this progression because the economic cost to us of disclaiming it is deemed too great.

The coronavirus crisis is horrific, but we must imagine a world ten or twenty years from now, in which the People's Republic of China's nominal Gross Domestic Product (GDP) is 50 percent larger than the United States. What power would an unconstrained communist China wield? What force of arms would they muster to intimidate and to control?

At the inception of America's entry into WWII, many strategists conjectured presciently that both Germany and Japan were destined to lose the war; their populations and their economies were too small, and their access to raw materials too tenuous, to be able to wage a protracted war against the Allies. Later, the Soviet Union posed a great challenge to our establishment of a post-war order conducive to international peace, development, and individual freedom.

Throughout the 1950s and early 1960s, CIA analysts predicted the Soviet economy would surpass America's, a prediction Soviet Premier Nikita Khrushchev often repeated. This calculus drove many American decisions. Arguably, the mistakes made by America in Southeast Asia were, in part, impelled by those errant estimates. The USSR never came close to matching the United States in economic output; today, America's GDP is at least twelve times Russia's.

China, however, is seemingly destined to outpace the United States in GDP during the next decade; indeed, China has plausibly already overtaken the United States, if GDP is measured by Purchasing Power Parity (PPP). Though China is far poorer than America in income per capita, its population is approximately 4.25 times larger than the United States. Thus, as China's per capita income grows to approximate that of developed nations, its total economic power will outstrip any rival state.

Adopting elements of the construct used by our country to rebuild Western Europe and Japan after World War II, four American actions, undertaken through an uninterrupted course of eight administrations, resulted in these significant steps aiding the ascent of the communist People's Republic of China: first, scientific aid to end famine in China (Norman Borlaug, Nobel Laureate, and the father of the Green Revolution, spent time working in China;[35] as a consequence of Borlaug's work, the land in Asia devoted to semi-dwarf rice and wheat types grew from 200 acres to forty million, helping to feed hundreds of millions of people on the continent); second, President Carter's diplomatic recognition of the People's Republic of China as China and his commitment to the United States government's engaging with reciprocal elements of the PRC; third, President Clinton's facilitation of the PRC's ultimate ascension to membership in the World Trade Organization (WTO) and his expansion of Chinese access to dual-use (civilian/military) technology;[36] and fourth, President Obama's embrace of the PRC as a non-adversarial peer state completed the PRC's envelopment of America's institutions and our modalities of power.

British economist Angus Maddison wrote, "China had been the world's biggest economy for nearly two millennia, but in the 1890s this position was taken by the United States. ...Chinese GDP per capita was lower in 1952 than in 1820, in stark contrast with experience elsewhere in the world economy. China's share of world GDP fell from a third to one twentieth. Its real per capita income fell from parity to a quarter of the world average."[37]

A substantial part of this precipitous economic decline can be attributed to the Opium Wars instigated by the British government. These campaigns forced the narcotics trade upon China and compromised, in various ways, the country's sovereignty. China's far more recent commerce in fentanyl is their "payback" for what the West did to it. The Treaty of Tientsin ended part of the Second Opium War: Great Britain, the United States, France, and Russia were parties to the asymmetrical documents comprising the treaty, which as ratified by the Chinese Emperor in 1860, further debased the country. China, today, views itself as more than a country: it is a civilization. From the Communist Party of China's perspective, the present turnabout in its power relationships is fair play, but to acknowledge this perspective must not engender our discounting the PRC's present threat to the world.

On September 25, 2015, the White House released its official statement on U.S.-China Economic Relations. The Obama White House statement revealed a disastrously flawed course. For example, this factsheet noted, "The U.S. side reiterated its commitment to encourage and facilitate exports of commercial high technology items to China for civilian-end users. Both sides commit to continue detailed and in-depth discussion of the export control issues of mutual interest within the U.S.-China High Technology and Strategic Trade Working Group."[38]

More troubling was the Obama Administration's enshrinement of Chinese goals with regard to industry penetration and co-option:

> The United States and China commit to limit the scope of their respective national security reviews of foreign investments (for the United States, the CFIUS process) solely to issues that constitute national security concerns, and not to generalize the scope of such reviews to include other broader public interest or economic issues. . . . When an investment poses a national security risk, the United States and China are to use their respective processes to address the risk as expeditiously as possible, including through targeted mitigation rather than prohibition whenever reasonably possible.[39]

The factsheet also limited America's capacity for correction when it announced, "Once an investment has completed the national security review process of either country, the investment generally should not be subject to review again if the parties close the investment as reviewed under the respective national security review process."[40]

The United States, in past conflicts, has been slow to anger. In confronting this present pandemic and the Chinese actions leading to it, fury, which is often fleeting, must be held in check, for it must be displaced by actions and policies to abate portions of the grave damage loosed on the world and enshrined by our past obsequiousness. In addition, any proper national strategy must peer into the future, to consider capabilities that must be attained, to meet threats yet unformed, but real.

Despite wrongs committed against China in the past, the People's Republic of China must not represent the future, for it is corrupt. Hearkening back to what Ronald Reagan did to spur the dissolution of the Union of Soviet Socialist Republics, the United States must enunciate that its objective is the peaceful end of the Communist Party of China. China existed for four thousand years before the formation of a communist junta within its borders; China can only achieve greatness combined with liberty and wealth if it frees itself from one-party rule and the despotism this type of government always brings.

ACTIONS:

- **Forge a consensus to adopt a new national strategy to address the unprecedented threat the People's Republic of China poses to America and to the world**
- **Declare the strategy and the cause in public fora**

CHAPTER TWO

THE PRESENT DANGER

It is logical to assume that after some initial point, Chinese political, military, and intelligence officials realized this outbreak of a new virus could be used as an economic weapon to bring down the economies of the West and thus assure Chinese hegemony. Given China's history of spawning new illnesses, China's political establishment must have had planning documents in place to serve the Communist Party of China's interests, should such a scenario of a novel virus spread unfold. Various stratagems to contain the spread in China, sow fear around the world, and involve certain elements of the legacy media and the elites of targeted countries, may be part of a broader, communist initiative. Manipulating data with regard to the virus would be central to any such operational plan.

On May 7, 2020, the Johns Hopkins University COVID-19 Dashboard, assembled by the Center for Systems Science and Engineering, using data accumulated by the Chinese, recorded the dead in Hubei Provence, whose capital is Wuhan, at 4,512, out of 4,637 for the entire country. According to Chinese authorities, 125 fatalities occurred in all other provinces, which comprise 1.38 billion people. A novel virus would go unrecognized for weeks. Indeed, China's own questionable records support this conjecture.

If the virus did experience exponential growth and doubled every day, in twenty-eight days it should have infected 268 million people. A one-percent mortality rate would thus result in millions of deaths, not fewer than 5,000. Of course, we do not know the true characteristics of the virus's spread. It clearly did not evolve in China in a manner suggestive of rapid, exponential growth. However, even if the PRC underreported its losses by a factor of ten or twenty or more, China's very low death and infection counts do not make sense. China was 124th in rank amongst nations as of late July 2020, as calculated by novel virus-related deaths per million of inhabitants per country. America was ninth.

Are there scenarios to explain these numbers? One explanation would involve an almost immediately recognized accidental release from the Wuhan Institute of Virology, engendering swift and firm containment procedures within China, but denied to the rest of the world by China's continuance of international travel from the virus's point of origin.

The second scenario is related but more cruel. Given China's research into biological warfare, it is conceivable a clandestine military or intelligence group within China sought to ensure supremacy through the acquisition of a naturally or seemingly naturally occurring virus that would be just transmissible and virulent enough to cause massive disruption in Western countries, but could be limited, given the regime's foreknowledge, within China. Such a virus could have been released accidentally or purposefully, with or without the knowledge of the PRC's most senior leadership. Allied intelligence must determine if either scenario took place, and if so, in what form.

Releases of biological warfare agents have occurred elsewhere. Perhaps the most infamous is the inadvertent leak of anthrax, in 1979, in Sverdlovsk, which killed sixty-four persons in that city, now called Ekaterinburg.[41] This release was acknowledged first in 1992 by Russian President Boris Yeltsin, who participated in the cover-up years earlier, when he was the communist party chief of that metropolis. In the intervening thirteen years between the disaster and the acknowledgment that the deaths were caused by agents developed for germ warfare, the international scientific community established no firm consensus as to what truly happened, for many believed the Soviet's disinformation campaign. While an engineered virus, resulting from manipulation done at the Wuhan Institute of Virology, must be considered unsupported by the present set of facts, without access to the lab, its data, and the initial sites of the spread, speculation does not equate to certain knowledge.

Abetting the PRC's denial of the access necessary for international investigators to determine the virus's genesis is the media's puerile argument that since the virus has been determined by independent studies of its genome to be of natural origin, it could not have come from the virology laboratory at Wuhan. This argument is wrong on two counts: first, definitive proof of the virus's origin and its evolution is not available due to the Communist Party of China's destruction of relevant materials and sites and its obstruction of international inquiries; second, by its own admission, and as is clearly communicated in its name, the state-controlled Wuhan Institute of Virology does study naturally occurring viruses.

ACTIONS:

- Determine by the joint action of allied intelligence agencies and through other means and investigations, the true genesis of COVID-19
- Document the acts of deception and instigation undertaken by the Communist Party of China to seed the virus; present this information to the world

CHAPTER THREE

CHALLENGES

The PRC represents a multidimensional threat encompassing all aspects of hard and soft power. Hard power is the use of coercion, monetary enticements, and force to attain policy goals; soft power is the result of attraction and co-option concerning outcomes, which become shared, to attain objectives supportive of interests. Until this pandemic, American soft power seemed destined to remain the dominant force in world affairs even as the PRC surpassed America's GDP.

Concurrent with the expectation of future Chinese economic preeminence, America's national debt and other competing priorities will serve to constrain U.S. military power. America's breadth of soft power was to be the barricade against these vectors. It was hoped our nation would withstand future Chinese economic might coupled with near military parity, for the United States would retain vast reservoirs of soft power, not possessed by other nations.

Our popular culture, our free press, and our multinational businesses have heretofore been liberalizing and democratizing forces, which have reflected America's supremacy in all major forms of soft power. The magnitude and the stability of this bulwark must be reconsidered; the PRC now wields substantial power in Hollywood and insinuates its control and propaganda into our press, our businesses, and our universities.

The PRC has transmuted aspects of America's soft power into that which is responsive to communist objectives. The means for this metamorphosis are America's freedoms, its laws, and its politicians, who are informed by the academy. Strategic purchases of U.S. businesses and the placement of Chinese companies on American stock exchanges and indexes have given the PRC enormous suasion over the avenues of American soft power.

The U.S.-China Economic and Security Review Commission has reported that as of February 25, 2019 there were 156 Chinese companies listed on the three largest U.S. exchanges. These firms had a combined capitalization of $1.2 trillion.

On May 20, 2020, the U.S. Senate approved, without objection, the bipartisan Holding Foreign Companies Accountable Act; it is now in the House of Representatives, having been introduced by Brad Sherman (D-CA). This legislation, if signed into law, could, in effect, force certain Chinese firms to be delisted from U.S. exchanges.

According to the official summary of this legislation,

> This bill requires certain issuers of securities to establish that they are not owned or controlled by a foreign government. Specifically, an issuer must make this certification if the Public Company Accounting Oversight Board [PCAOB] is unable to audit specified reports because the issuer has retained a foreign public accounting firm not subject to inspection by the board. Furthermore, if the board is unable to inspect the issuer's public accounting firm for three consecutive years, the issuer's securities are banned from trade on a national exchange or through other methods.[42]

Thus, in effect, Chinese companies would be compelled to use public accounting firms inspected by the PCAOB, after an initial period of required disclosures, to be made if a business is not presently in compliance with this requirement. This is very important; to be most meaningful, however, we should implore the U.K. to follow our Senate's lead and to enact similar measures to protect Britain's financial markets.

Through investment and by direct and indirect pressure, the PRC, in its various forms, has influenced America's most important media companies. These media companies, in turn, own major news networks, services, and publishing houses. An example of Chinese power in Hollywood is contained in the movie sequel *Top Gun: Maverick*. In the original 1986 film, Maverick's iconic bomber jacket displayed military patches including both Japanese and Taiwanese flags.

In the new movie, a film made possible through the cooperation of the U.S. Navy, these flags are replaced with meaningless patches rendered in similar colors to obscure what was done.[43] Citing this example, Senator Ted Cruz has introduced the SCRIPT Act to halt Pentagon assistance to companies whose films are censored in service to Chinese demands.[44]

The PRC's insertion into Hollywood has a model: during the 1930s, Hollywood studio films were subjected to German censorship or cancellation so the studios could retain access to the German market, which before World War II was the second largest in the world. It is critical to note this censorship affected American films shown not just in Germany, but worldwide.

Hollywood, in effect, cooperated with the German government during the decade before World War II; the studios did this to protect their business interests. A film almost lost to history, by Cornelius Vanderbilt Jr., *Hitler's Reign of Terror*, premièred at one independent cinema in 1934;[45] the Vanderbilt film was stopped from future distribution due to Nazi pressure and it was never picked up by a studio. *Confessions of a Nazi Spy*, released in 1939, was the first truly anti-Nazi studio film.[46]

The damage Nazis sought in Hollywood and in Los Angeles would have incontestably been greater had attorney Leon Lawrence Lewis,[47] the first national secretary of the Anti-Defamation League, not created an anti-Nazi spy network in 1933. Secretly supported by studio executives, Lewis was able to place his group's spies within local Nazi and fascist groups, passing critical information to FBI and military intelligence offices.

This is complex history we must remember, for it is crucial as it provides the context for the PRC's penetration and its mechanisms of control in today's Hollywood. Only now, the control exercised by a foreign power has far greater reach, for today's media conglomerates that own the film and television studios also own major news networks.[48] Therefore, to maintain access to the Chinese market for film and television, there exists, if not substantial pressure, the business context to manipulate and to bowdlerize news in America to curry favor with China.

We face information warfare on a level never experienced. This battle, moreover, has been waged almost entirely in one direction: against the United States. Misled by the majority of our press, we, as a society, have entered a palace of mirrors, each distorting the image of what is real. It is, therefore, critical to understand how many persons perceive the present crisis as hyperreal, in the sense its predominant narrative, which postulates no intrinsic Chinese governmental culpability, has supplanted the true nature of this pandemic.

This has occurred because the narrative has been shaped by sources controlled by the Communist Party of China, which are amplified by sympathetic or unwitting members of the media in the West. The created narrative is thus more real to the public, due to its narrative strength, than is the actual situation. Cyberwarfare is another agent. Without the immediate dissemination of veridical information, errant public-policy decisions are bound to follow.

In the years leading up to WWII, strong business relationships with Germany and Japan prevented the free countries of the West from acting decisively to forestall German and Japanese aggression. Public sentiment to avoid future wars, after the losses in the Somme and in Verdun, held sway. Now, the economic and business pressures for America and its allies to foreswear meaningful action against the PRC are as great as can be imagined.

To act decisively to limit Chinese exploitation and adventurism portends economic strife and the end of a globalist international order that has existed for fifty years. We must, however, put ourselves to the question: Do we have a choice?

If the intelligence services of the United States and its allies find proof that the PRC—knowing the virus had initially spread from its virology lab in Wuhan, or emanated from some other source, such as the city's wet market— locked down travel to other parts of China while permitting international transport from this city, at the time the Communist Party of China prevented international fact finding, this state committed what amounts to a war crime. If this is proved, then inaction is an invitation for repetition or mimicry, for the path to disassemble America is manifest. Without a response measured to this assault, we will show weakness and undermine deterrence.

ACTIONS:

- Recognize the nature of the PRC's multidimensional threat, no matter the near-term cost
- Take decisive, bipartisan action to limit the PRC's misappropriation of elements of American soft power
- Provide the public with highly accurate and timely information about the coronavirus and the PRC's role in the present disaster
- Pass the Holding Foreign Companies Accountable Act; support similar measures in the U.K. and elsewhere
- Deny the PRC access to American media companies, especially those controlling news networks; pass the SCRIPT Act

CHAPTER FOUR

RECALIBRATION

Even without specific reference to China, the present pandemic makes clear America must adopt a manifold of new initiatives to better protect against biological as well as chemical and nuclear threats, including electromagnetic pulse weapons and radiological agents. Possibly more destructive than a pandemic would be a failure of our power grid resulting in a protracted black-sky event, in which electricity is no longer available from our established infrastructure. This can be caused by cyberterrorism, by an electromagnetic pulse, or by kinetic damage to key nodes.

Heretofore, the U.S. government considered the consequences of a pandemic in abstract terms; we have lacked the institutional structures and vocabulary to institute needed actions, even when significant intelligence was at hand. Resulting from multiple visits to the virology lab in Wuhan by a U.S. delegation, detailed Department of State cables in 2018 warned of substantial safety issues.[49]

These reports, however, caused no meaningful action although the potential transmissibility of the bat-borne viruses, studied at the lab, and the ramifications of such transference to persons, were the focus of acute concern in the scientific community. What was missing for this intelligence to have made a difference, in order to avert a future, worldwide crisis, was an established pathway and bureaucracy to permit the time-urgent transmission of such information to decision-making authorities at the highest levels of government.

The creation of such avenues for information and decision-making is a complex task, for the duplication of existing bureaucratic elements can be worse than no action at all. Therefore, the president should engage a special taskforce to map existing, relevant governmental structures and to recommend a new system, which would be robust, anticipatory, investigative, and responsive to a spectrum of future threats in this domain. Part of the solution must be the creation of interagency groups to speed intelligence and threat assessments to senior officials in order to promote rapid and preventative action.

Another strand that must be realized is the modern replication of WWII's War Production Board to ensure a measure of autarky in the production of a range of medicines and related raw ingredients. Domestic production of critical medical devices must also be pursued, with consideration given to the enactment of targeted, multiyear tax cuts and other incentives for American companies repatriating production from China.

In the case of medicines and medical equipment, supply vulnerability studies must be instituted to determine the net levels of domestic and allied manufacture necessary to ensure supplies of these goods in a time of emergency. The 1984 National Security Council Stockpile/Industrial Mobilization Planning Study, one of the largest investigations of its kind, can provide a template for the required interagency analysis and recommendations. During WWII, the War Production Board brought together cabinet officials and the CEOs of major U.S. corporations to ensure the extraordinarily rapid expansion of war-related production. From 1940 to 1943, aircraft production increased fourteen-fold. This was accomplished, in part, through the introduction of a Controlled Materials Plan, which allocated, through a system of preferences, key materials to designated industries and factories, guaranteed the unhindered production of required armaments. Today, employing such a public-private structure, would expedite rapid increases in domestic production of medications and equipment being attained.

ACTIONS:

- Attain the time-urgent transmission of critical intelligence, with regard to disease propagation, through the creation of new organizational structures within government

- Create the capacity to cope with biological, chemical, and nuclear threats as well as EMP and black-sky events

- Require production of our medicines, medical supplies, and equipment be returned to the United States or to allied countries, which possess secure sources of supply and transport; propose multiyear tax cuts and other incentives to speed change

- Establish the capability, based on our WWII experience, to facilitate public-private management structures in times of emergency, which may be buttressed by preferential allocations of critical materials, to enable the production of essential medicines, machinery, products, or other needed articles

CHAPTER FIVE

BELT AND ROAD

Concomitant with the PRC's insertion into our system of higher education, our economy, our media, and our core businesses, China has embarked on a global strategy constituting a new imperialism. The PRC's Belt and Road Initiative (BRI) seeks to shape connectivity and alliances on a global scale, which may include sixty-five other countries comprising 30 percent of global GDP and 75 percent of established energy reserves.[50] China's aggressive parlay in the construction of various types of power plants throughout the developing world is recognized as being inextricably tied to the BRI and is, for the PRC, imperative.

China and Russia appropriate national assets worldwide through loaded energy and development deals. This drive is only enhanced by the pandemic if no countervailing action ensues. In Djibouti, China holds 77 percent of the debt.[51] In Venezuela, Russia received 49.9 percent of Citgo in 2016 as collateral for $1.5 billion in cash.[52] Kenya, Angola, Nigeria, and Zambia were all on the cusp of asset appropriation before the present crisis.

Estimates indicate China lent African nations $124 billion from 2000 through 2016. Presently, the Kiel Institute for the World Economy values Chinese loans to developing nations at $520 billion,[53] an extraordinary sum. Yet, as destabilizing as these acquisitive loans are, the true situation may be far more dire.

Dr. Christoph Trebesch, author of the Kiel study, contends a tremendous amount of Chinese lending is "hidden."[54] This may amount to an additional half trillion dollars or more of indebtedness to China by impoverished countries. If so, these amounts may, indeed, dwarf the funds lent by the World Bank and the International Monetary Fund.

The largest portion of each loan made by the PRC may not be provided generally to the borrower but spent in China to finance Chinese-made inputs and trained labor. The recipient country is, in effect, financing jobs and manufacturing in China. Worse still, the ultimate result for targeted countries is to have their assets expropriated, due to loan nonperformance, which the PRC may purposely contrive as the hidden tenet of each transaction.

Given the PRC's actions in this domain, its loans to developing nations must, as a matter of U.S policy, be turned from being a pillar of coercion into an albatross. Great Britain and India are leaders of the fifty-four-member-state Commonwealth of Nations:[55] this constellation of countries, which stretches across the globe, should be mobilized into a powerful alternative to the PRC's exploitative model of development.

The creation of the Commonwealth of Nations in the last century is a stunning achievement, whose offices and whose members can play vital roles in the accomplishment of sustainable and equitable growth in developing countries. The transition of the British Empire into the Commonwealth of Nations and the Commonwealth realm is unmatched in its scope in world history with the exception of the transmutation of the Western Roman Empire into the Roman Catholic Church. Saint Augustine wrote *The City of God* in response to the Roman public's outcry over the Visigoths' sacking of Rome in AD 410.[56] This book is recognized as foundational to Western religious and moral thought.

To Augustine, the ruination of Rome as an ephemeral City of Man was surmounted completely by Christianity's triumph in the form of the establishment of the eternal City of God. The concept of dioceses as administrative domains within the Roman Empire preceded the term's ecclesiastical use. After the establishment of Christianity as the official state religion of the empire in the fourth century AD, bishops and priests were emplaced alongside the provincial governors and the bureaucrats of the Empire. As the Western Empire withered and collapsed, all that was left were the offices of the Church, which were formed as a reduplicate of the Roman administrative state.

The expansion and solidification of the Commonwealth of Nations as a substitute for the British Empire, albeit appreciably weakened in terms of British influence, had as its model, Augustine's City of God. It is this deeply rooted history and record of associations of the Commonwealth of Nations that make it a viable alternative to China's BRI.

New insights and mechanisms must be wrought for such a substitution to be successful. Disruptive innovation is designed to attract new constituents beyond an entity's normal markets or range of actions and operations. Importantly, it is this concept, taken from the business world, which undergirds many of Donald Trump's actions in today's political sphere. Disruptive innovation may be used to facilitate new initiatives and programs within the member states of the Commonwealth of Nations.

President Trump, in his scope of actions involving NATO, terrorism, immigration, trade, North Korea, Israel, the Middle East, and China, has demonstrated his belief that disruptive innovation must be expanded throughout our conduct of foreign affairs. Established political entities, such as the Communist Party of China and the regime's ministries, branches, and intelligence operations, which are fortified by their domains of competence, are highly susceptible to constituency erosion if a rival political actor innovates through disruption. This is the paramount threat Donald Trump poses. We must, therefore, be watchful of reprisals either overt or clandestine, mounted by China and, conceivably, by internal forces from within the United States and our allies that may imperil the initiatives we mount to oppose this juggernaut.

ACTIONS:

- Undertake determined efforts to deny China's Belt and Road Initiative, especially in Africa
- Inform the governments and the elites of developing nations as to the nature and the extent of Chinese and Russian predatory lending
- Turn the colossal extent of the PRC's loans to developing countries against the Communist Party of China
- Extend alternate terms to key nations on the brink of asset appropriation due to China's rapaciousness
- Advance a substitute to the BRI; cooperate in this endeavor with Britain and with India
- Marshal support for these initiatives from the member states of the Commonwealth of Nations

CHAPTER SIX

POWER AND INFORMATION

The production, distribution, and use of electricity, during the next several decades, will undergo a transformation more profound than any experienced since the time of Edison. Power, information, and communications will fuse. Electrical distribution lines will be transformed into channels moving energy and information multi-directionally. New power stations, coupled with smart electric grids, will be foundational to this transformation.

The real-time delivery and use of electricity and information, encompassing all data related to supply and demand, will permit optimality in resource allocation and investment. Such efficiency is impossible without a spectrum of newly developed technologies.

These technologies, taken as a whole, constitute the smart grid, an intelligent electricity distribution network, designed to meet the precise needs of system participants. The information layer of the smart grid will contain business process data critical for industrial competitiveness in the twenty-first century. Electricity, connectivity, social media, and access to large stores of information nourish the foundations for freedom.

Historically, conflicts arise from perceived inequalities or differential birth rates among adjacent groups, competition for constrained resources, religious differences, or the desire to change the political order in support of a construct, perceived by its adherents to be utopian. The provision of electricity, coupled with the concomitant exchange of information, can undercut these threats, but only if such initiatives are supported by optimized resource allocation within market economies.

In free societies, the development of new sources of energy boosts economic development in areas that may be destitute or barren, enhances class mobility through individual progress, permits environmental and water conservation through enhanced knowledge networks. It accelerates precision farming through the mastery of information and the provision of power, and supports human enhancement and comity through the sharing of experiences. The equitable attainment of electricity will soon be recognized as a basic human need, for without it, knowledge, personal potential, and rights are thwarted.

Of special concern, therefore, is China's and Russia's building of nuclear power plants internationally, which may be coupled with smart electric grids, for the goals of these states do not support the humanitarian objectives enumerated. China has forty-five nuclear power reactors in operation domestically and twelve under construction; the nation's plans call for the building of thirty more plants in key countries and regions in the next twenty years.[57] Russia has thirty-eight nuclear power reactors in operation at home and has contracts or plans to build at least twenty in foreign countries.

According to the Carnegie Endowment for International Peace, China is responsible for more than half of new global investments in nuclear power.[58] If China transitions to fast-neutron reactors, which recycle large quantities of plutonium fuel, their potential for worldwide dominance increases. The leadership of China understands fully that for a world in search of low-carbon energy, fission power represents the chief viable avenue for at least the next forty years. This constitutes a potential market opportunity that will, almost certainly, exceed one trillion dollars.

Nations in the Middle East, Africa, the Indian subcontinent, and Asia should be offered a multinational, free-market alternative to nuclear plants built by China or by Russia. Invigorated efforts, by a consortium of allied powers, in the provision of fission plants to interested countries must be part of a new strategy enshrining low-carbon energy and joint security in an alternative form to Chinese or to Russian designs.

The safety of new plants must be a primary concern: project technology, quality, fuel-cycle protection, maintenance, education, and defense should be peerless. These are attributes Chinese or Russian technology and operation can never provide.

Nuclear power generation occurs in a tripartite world of plant construction: China and Russia each constitute a dominion. The last dominion is made up of every other country building or capable of building nuclear power plants.

Failure to combine the multifaceted abilities of corporations and institutions will doom each individual western nation's nuclear power industry to failure in competing against the state-sponsored enterprises of China or Russia. Only a concerted offensive—deploying a multinational business framework engaging and linking participating states and private companies in an international consortium—will allow the west to prevail in the new nuclear power race. Such a consortium, realized throughout the globe, if built and controlled by free nations, will become an apex industry, fusing information technologies with the production and distribution of energy, in modes supportive of environmental, economic, and security imperatives.

China's and Russia's Loan, Build, Seize development model for national projects such as nuclear power plants is disreputable. The acquisitive development strategies short-change stakeholders outside China or Russia. Projects built by China or Russia are dependent on rigid supervision from afar, suspect safety regimes, inferior technology, lack of quality control, and proper administration.

China and Russia offer limited educational and training opportunities for the citizens of purchasing nations. The defensive systems for nuclear plants built by China or Russia are backward and subject to failure or defeat. The fuel-cycle management for these projects is exploitive and locks purchasing nations into unalterable, life-of-plant terms.

During the British Raj in the Indian subcontinent, which lasted from 1858 to 1947, Britain built cantonment churches, which resembled normal places of worship, but were, in fact, dual-use structures that could be transformed into forts during periods of insurrection. Chinese and Russian power plants, built all over the world, inherently have the ability to be employed as redoubts for Chinese and Russian military forces. They are thus tools for instability and suzerainty.

World population will grow to 8.2 billion by 2025; this addition of almost a half-billion persons makes precise resource management a necessity. This is particularly so in developing states in which birth rates are very high. Median estimates for world population are 8.6 billion in 2030, and 9.8 billion in 2050.

With such unprecedented increases, abundant electricity and information can dampen the inculcation of enmities among peoples, which feed on perceptions of waste and inequality. Indeed, intelligent governance will have better prospects to take root in enriched environments; this will promote conflict resolution and the adoption of nonviolent means of intercession.

ACTIONS:

• **Lead in the creation of low-carbon sources of energy and smart grids, which will carry electricity and information to meet emergent needs**

• **Contest China's and Russia's present dominance in the construction and in the management of nuclear plants beyond their borders**

• **Organize free nations to form a consortium of companies, to build safe and secure nuclear plants around the world, to provide electricity future populations will require**

• **Remind young people worldwide, Russia's greatest gift to the Ukrainian people was a nuclear reactor at Chernobyl**

CHAPTER SEVEN

TARGETED STATES

If the West slides into steep recession, developing nations—deprived of their ability to sell raw materials to the United States and to Europe, and faced with many developmental loans they will have no ability to repay—may sell whatever they can in national riches to China for cents on the dollar. The Chinese Belt and Road Initiative will thus be realized surreptitiously and consummately from a communist viewpoint. Yet, it is this avarice that is the PRC's Achilles' heel.

America must exploit this weakness by offering African and developing nations an alternative to the BRI. The assembly of such nations to spur contestation must be a central component of a new U.S. national strategy. To effect this, America must exploit China's susceptibility to client-state erosion. To end-run China, America and its allies must innovate disruptively, support capitalistic principles, and marshal a spectrum of hard and soft power to unseat the PRC from its perches in developing nations.

Should America continue to be locked down in some form, for an extended period of time, the unintended consequences will be massive and may inflict more damage than the virus. Developing nations, deprived of revenue from the sale of their commodities and goods to developed nations, will surely suffer catastrophic losses and many deaths due to inadequate income to provide for proper nutrition and healthcare. Such a scarcity in available food, when coupled with sub-Saharan health systems, which in many countries spend one-hundredth as much per capita as does the United States, will yield catastrophic consequences, with countries' healthcare systems possibly being overwhelmed by both the coronavirus and by other diseases.

The plight of developing nations is perhaps the strongest reason why America must overturn its past relationship with China. Looking forward, by the year 2100, seventeen of the world's most populous cities, comprising approximately 700 million people, will be in sub-Saharan Africa.[59] If ample electricity is not available, mass migration, war, religious extremism, and new pandemics will result. The cost to the world's nations will be measured in the tens of trillions of dollars.

If a pestilence as virulent as Ebola spreads globally, it may take the planet decades to recover. The challenges Africa faces will be replicated across the world. China has exploited this overwhelming need and challenge for its own advantage, thus ensuring its own development, as opposed to its assistance to other nations.

Immense, densely populated urban areas must have electricity for the desalination and the provision of water, precision farming, jobs, governance, and human advancement. America and its allies must offer reliable, scalable alternatives to carbon fuels, which often consist of the open burning of wood or coal in less economically developed countries. Such open, unfiltered sources of energy create massive quantities of black carbon, causing severe pollution and disease, in contrast to modern, coal-fueled power plants employing technologies to mitigate pollution.

A range of development projects to include renewable energy, secure thermoelectric plants, and smart electric grids must be proffered as a substitute for the PRC's model of Loan, Build, Seize; only America and its allies can provide an alternative means of progress for poor countries. Ceding this ground to China or to Russia can only ensure the continued impoverishment of nations currently experiencing the highest birthrates in human history.

Poverty and burgeoning, urbanized populations are substrates for future pandemics perhaps far more virulent than COVID-19. Cabinet officials from the Departments of State, Treasury, Defense, Justice, and Energy, supported by our intelligence community, and by other agencies, must convene interagency groups to develop a set of initiatives to undermine and to replace the BRI.

ACTIONS:

- Expose the PRC's greed in its acquisitions of the national assets of developing countries through China's deployment of its model of Loan, Build, Seize

- Form an assembly of developing states to oppose China's tactics of resource and asset acquisition

- Disrupt the PRC's usurpation of developing countries by creating new alternatives that suppress recipient corruption and fulfill societal needs through free market principles and innovation

- Convene cabinet-level meetings, supported by new interagency groups, to establish policies and programs to suppress China's external, developmental ambitions

CHAPTER EIGHT

INTELLIGENCE

Of all the forces in the world today, only weapons of mass destruction (WMDs), disease, and the PRC can meaningfully affect our nation's course. It follows, therefore, these three specters should dominate the efforts of America's intelligence community. Terrorism (that does not involve potential WMDs), Russia, the Democratic People's Republic of Korea, and Iran are secondary in their ability to damage the United States.

If China did, indeed, prohibit internal travel from Wuhan while permitting international flights, such information should have been conveyed immediately to U.S. national authorities, but it remains far from certain such a transfer of intelligence took place. Updated tasking and bureaucratic structures are required to institute new collection priorities.

The Director of National Intelligence should be charged by the president to study, report, and institute a government-wide recalibration of our intelligence assets to support the reordering of our priorities. Publicly, the Director of National Intelligence must proffer an elaboration of new, allied measures to counteract the virus-related subterfuge propagated by China and its information operations aimed at misdirecting public opinion in free societies.

Counterintelligence must also be a priority. The incipient nature of Chinese appropriation is difficult to contest. Much of it relies on Chinese financial power, coupled with a belligerent type of soft power referred to as sharp power. Classical disinformation operations, undertaken using an array of social media platforms, are coupled with "or else" stratagems that relay consequences for countervailing actions, in order to instill passivity that targets the weakest nodes antagonistic to Chinese aims.

As a nation, we must instill a new level of insight concerning Chinese intelligence operations. Successful intelligence operatives act counterintuitively in ways contrary to the expectations of ordinary persons: this is the essence of the craft, but such modes of thinking are alien to most businesspeople. Intelligence operatives manifest the ability to be chimeric, to adjust rapidly to new situations. They do this to survive.

Operatives think nonlinearly, for the past must be made malleable to conform to the needs of the present. The creation of unreal histories is common in Chinese information operations. Therefore, increased engagement and threat briefings by U.S. intelligence agents and contractors to America's businesses must be emphasized. The creation of online threat briefings, available to U.S. businesses, is imperative.

The PRC reportedly uses artificial intelligence (AI) to support decision and game theory to prioritize its intelligence efforts. These techniques were developed in the United States but are not generally employed in decision-making by America's most senior leaders. This must change.

A support structure for mathematically based decision and game theory must be established in the White House.

Consequential decisions and strategies should be the subject of several independent analyses: first, the descriptive and referential analysis; second, the aforementioned AI-supported examination. The Cabinet must be presented with both.

This more rigorous approach to decision-making should be harnessed to support counterintelligence operations directed at the PRC's penetrative tactics. With AI, there is the potential to counterpunch in near-real time.

ACTIONS:

- **Reorder America's intelligence priorities: make the emergence of disease, the PRC, and WMDs the top intelligence targets**

- **Require the DNI to undertake the realignment of our nation's intelligence priorities; this restructuring should be documented in classified and in public reports**

- **Direct the DNI to release a public catalogue of measures to be taken by American and allied informational agencies to counteract China's blatantly false narratives relating to COVID-19**

- **Instruct America's intelligence-related agencies to mount information operations to counter Chinese efforts in this domain**

- **Authorize enhanced threat briefings for businesses by U.S. intelligence agents and contractors; create online briefings that inform about the range of PRC intelligence operations directed at U.S. companies**

- **Build the capacity to employ AI-supported analyses to support decision-making at the highest levels of government**

CHAPTER NINE

BUSINESS OR THEFT

Any response to China's transgressions must hold trade as a central concern. Almost nothing affects the PRC more than changes in trade policy. Trade imbalances and China's theft of intellectual property must be addressed by using an array of policy levers. Economist Albert Hirschman wrote in 1945, "A country trying to make the most out of its strategic position with respect to its own trade will try precisely to create conditions which make the interruption of trade of much graver concern to its trading partners than to itself."[60] Most cases alleging harmful trade practices involve Section 201 (domestic injury) or Section 301 (unfair foreign practices) of the U.S. Trade Act of 1974.

To develop a new paradigm supportive of the American worker and, therefore, inimical to China, resolute action must be taken, for America's 2019 trade deficit with China reached $345.6 billion. What is not commonly noted is this trade deficit does not include intellectual property (IP) theft by China and by other nations. Total losses of this type to the U.S. economy far exceed two trillion dollars in the last ten years alone.

Expressing this theft in relatable terms, this sum could have made two million American families instant millionaires. Such loss estimates are conservative: IP theft does incalculable harm in reducing incentives for U.S. companies to invest in research and development, for it makes little sense to invest in something that will be stolen.

Due to the magnitude of IP theft, individual cases are too numerous to list, but the effects are devastating; for example, AMSC, a U.S. firm which developed proprietary code for clean energy solutions, suffered a dramatic decline in its stock price, a precipitous loss in its business, and a massive reduction of jobs when a Chinese company, Sinovel (one of the world's largest wind-turbine businesses), stole AMSC software and then refused shipment of millions in AMSC product Sinovel ordered before the theft. The Department of Justice acted against Sinovel.

According to the 2018 Department of Justice press release,

> A manufacturer and exporter of wind turbines based in the People's Republic of China was sentenced today for stealing trade secrets from AMSC, a U.S.-based company formerly known as American Superconductor Inc. . . . The Court found that AMSC's losses from the theft exceeded $550 million, and imposed the maximum statutory fine in the amount of $1.5 million on Sinovel Wind Group LLC. The Court found that the parties settled the restitution amount, and imposed a year of probation until Sinovel pays the full restitution amount.[61]

Losses to U.S. competitiveness are certainly immense and take many forms: in 2011, 75 percent of China's $12 billion domestic software market was satisfied by pirated software, much of it stolen from American companies. Due to this, Chinese PC business-related software spending was

7 percent of comparable U.S. software spending. This conveys massive competitive advantages to Chinese firms and entrepreneurs.

Another aspect of IP theft is system compromise. The Terminal High Altitude Area Defense (THAAD) antiballistic missile and the P-8 anti-submarine warfare aircraft, along with other U.S. weapon systems, have been found to contain counterfeit parts that may reduce mission performance. According to former Democratic Senator Carl Levin, "There is a flood of counterfeits and it is putting our military men at risk and costing us a fortune."[62] The range and methods employed by the Chinese deemphasize blatant, transparent thefts, governmental involvement, and insertions, but have increased in their sophistication and breadth.

The cessation of Chinese IP theft will require a concentrated effort and new modalities by the U.S. government working with American industry, yet such action would yield enormous benefits, and if coupled with synchronous actions by allied governments, the PRC would be impinged, but would have no avenue of complaint. As an initial step, the NATO countries, Australia, Japan, and the Republic of Korea should develop the means to rapidly pass intelligence between them regarding industries and companies possessing key technologies believed to be at risk or have been targeted by China according to intelligence sources.

A multilateral initiative of this type is foundational to success in this difficult and contested sphere. Affected countries can then work with businesses to halt illicit transfers. In terms of counterfeited items, with particular concern for the compromise of military equipment through the unintended incorporation of Chinese-made parts, a system of etching, lithography, and secret coding by time, date, and place of manufacture may secure each part and thus inhibit Chinese infiltration and the compromise of our military systems.

The 2013 IP Commission Report prepared by former Director of National Intelligence Admiral Dennis Blair and by Ambassador John Huntsman stated the following measure be considered in the context of IP theft, "if the loss of IP continues at current levels" and other remedial actions fail, "Recommend that Congress and the administration impose a tariff on all Chinese-origin imports, designed to raise 150% of all U.S. losses from Chinese IP theft in the previous year, as estimated by the secretary of commerce."[63]

U.S. imports from China in 2019 amounted to $452.2 billion, resulting in a net trade deficit of $345.6 billion. Assuming IP losses due to China of $270 billion for 2019, the imposition of the suggested tariff would yield $405 billion in revenue, wiping away the entire trade deficit, if trade continues at present levels. In actuality, however, tariffs at these levels would reduce trade substantially, which the PRC fears.

In our consideration of IP theft, we must not overlook direct efforts to infiltrate or to co-opt. Mathematician, aerospace engineer, and nuclear physicist Hsue-Shen Tsien, born in Shanghai, was educated at MIT and then recruited to work at the California Institute of Technology and the Jet Propulsion Laboratory. As a scientist, he participated in the creation of the first atomic bomb as part of the Manhattan Project. Hsue-Shen Tsien was later stripped of his security clearances due to concerns he was a communist and a spy and in 1951 was declared subject to deportation. Subsequently, Hsue-Shen Tsien was allegedly traded for American pilots, captured during the Korean War.

Upon his arrival in China, Hsue-Shen Tsien became the architect of China's atomic bomb program. Later, he became known as the "Father of Chinese Rocketry" for his work in the development of the Dongfeng ballistic missile;[64] the fruits of Hsue-Shen Tsien's work and associations now undergird North Korea's nuclear and ballistic-missile programs. Unfortunately, this type of case is not unique. Thus, prevention of the PRC's exfiltration of defense, high-technology, and energy-related data has to become the first priority of the Counterintelligence Division of the National Security Branch of the Federal Bureau of Investigation.

To address the trade imbalance and IP theft, asymmetric responses must then be gamed and pathways found. The arsenal of American policy tools may then be leveraged in a systematic way, which minimizes deleterious consequences. Preservation of our technological base requires we enact severe limits on PRC graduate students in all Science, Technology, Engineering, and Mathematics (STEM) subjects. Therefore, we should rescind, where possible, any grant funding to students from the PRC. In addition, all Confucius Institutes at American universities should be shuttered until they be stripped of their propagandistic mission.

The exception for national security reasons to the presumption in favor of free trade is embodied in the World Trade Organization as well as our nation's trade laws. Contracting nations to the WTO have recognized the requirement for independent defense and security measures, which need to be exempt from general legal obligations: the WTO incorporates Article XXI of GATT 1994, which provides for national security exemptions.

The president can expand his use of Section 232 findings (as specified in the Trade Expansion Act of 1962), which require the president to determine whether imports "threaten to impair the national security."[65] As an immediate measure to effect a level of self-sufficiency with regard to domestic medical production, Section 232 could be employed to ensure a specified level of the nation's supply (net of exports) be provided by domestic or allied sources for drugs and medical products.

There have been calls, in the wake of this pandemic, for the United States to abandon the WTO, which succeeded the General Agreement on Tariffs and Trade (GATT). It is premature for the United States to leave an organization that has embodied our principles and has its root in our establishment of a world order in the aftermath of WWII. China has abused the WTO's policy that permits countries to self-identify as developing nations. The PRC, second only to the United States in economic output, has declared itself to be a developing nation and thus is the beneficiary of WTO rules designed to assist such countries. This must end.

The United States, working with allied nations, must attempt to reform the WTO, to constrain China's abuse of the WTO's principles and agreements, which were designed to promote free trade and fairness. Only if America does not succeed, should we consider the abandonment of an international organization we did so much to create and nurture, and should the need to abandon the WTO come to pass, our exit must not be unilateral.

To address trade imbalances with China, a comprehensive list must be assembled of the policy tools, laws, illicit practices, customs, inducements, and regulations China uses to spur trade. Such information should be at hand from the United States intelligence community and from other offices of government. Responses must be wrought using decision analyses to shape strategy.

In the wake of the present pandemic, President Trump must declare the magnitude of IP losses to the U.S. He must state America has heretofore expended little meaningful effort to eliminate such theft. Thus, the president must enforce fair and reciprocal trade, which takes full account of the PRC's goals. Congress must act in a bipartisan manner to grant the president expanded trade tools, which answer China's threat to our national security and economy.

ACTIONS:

- Oppose Chinese IP theft in all its forms
- Explicate that China's economic expansion would have been impossible without their theft of American technology; produce and distribute lists of technologies and products stolen or copied by China; urge other countries to do the same
- Make the numbers relevant: explain how the U.S. has lost enough from IP theft to have made two million American families instant millionaires
- Target counterfeit parts and assemblies, which may compromise critical machinery or weapon systems; institute tagging measures to ensure genuineness
- Lead the NATO nations, Australia, Japan, and the Republic of Korea in the collection and the dissemination of business-specific information related to IP theft and countermeasures
- Institute punishing tariffs against the PRC if IP theft persists
- Initiate comprehensive controls to prevent the stealing of data, by foreign agents, from our defense, high-technology, and energy-related industrial base; order the FBI to make such IP theft the top priority of its Counterintelligence Division, and put into law criminal penalties for any American company or individual that shares proprietary or sensitive information with China, which pertains to these matters
- Limit strictly the opportunities for students from the PRC to study the STEM subjects at the graduate level
- Employ Section 232 findings to shore up our medically related industries

- Develop a comprehensive, publicly available inventory of China's unfair trade practices and the tools it uses to achieve its aims
- Reform the WTO or leave it along with other U.S. allies

CHAPTER TEN

COUNTERBALANCE

To name but five American businesses under full or partial Chinese ownership is to demonstrate the penetration of our economy by large Chinese companies. Motorola Mobility and IBM's personal computer division have been acquired by Lenovo;[66] Smithfield Foods, the world's largest pork producer, is owned by the WH Group;[67] Legendary Pictures Productions, LLC, is owned by the Wanda Group,[68] which also has held a significant stake in AMC Theatres, the largest chain in America.[69]

Combined efforts to stem IP theft will have little long-term effect unless they are married with measures to prohibit or to take back the PRC's ownership of key U.S. and allied businesses, which may have been facilitated through the use of proxies or front companies. The Committee on Foreign Investment in the United States (CFIUS), a senior multiagency group chaired by the secretary of the treasury, is charged with the responsibility to determine if the security implications of foreign investments disqualify pending mergers or acquisitions of American companies or their operations. The Exon–Florio Amendment (50 U.S.C. app 2170) was signed into law by President Reagan and grants the president the authority to block any investment or acquisition if a "foreign interest exercising control might take action that threatens to impair the national security."[70] CFIUS was designated by President Reagan as the bureaucratic mechanism that serves this decision process. Unlike the processes employed by many other countries, CFIUS is not directly chartered to review business transactions threatening to harm the American economy or its workers, though there has been movement in this sphere.

President Trump signed the Foreign Investment Risk Review Modernization Act (FIRRMA) into law in 2018.[71] FIRRMA essentially enlarged the scope of CFIUS to include consideration of a transaction's impact on U.S. manufacturing, competitiveness, and the protection of transformative technologies. The transactions now assessed include not only acquisitions, but licenses, sales, real estate, minority holdings, and stakes in venture capital or private equity funds. The expanded compass of CFIUS is critical, but more must be done.

To chart an enhanced course for CFIUS, the world's nations should be categorized into five tiers. Kept classified, these groupings would comprise Allied, Friendly, Non-Aligned, Adversarial, and Belligerent nations. The latter two categories should be preclusive, in most circumstances, of ownership or of significant minority positions in U.S. enterprises. Present circumstances argue for a determination that the PRC is, indeed, an adversarial state.

One of our first actions in this sphere must be the prohibition, in the United States and across the world, of the deployment of Huawei's 5G networks, systems, phones, and devices. It should be considered obvious that tools for espionage, industrial and otherwise, can be implanted in these systems and apparatuses.

Depending on the final U.S. government verdict on Chinese responsibility for the spread of the virus, America might demand reparations; if so, such reparations should be scaled not as a function of the ravages of the disease, but as a function of the Communist Party of China's duplicity in their presentation of the facts concerning the genesis of the disease, its evolution, its spread, and the party's alleged acts to hoard personal protective equipment and to limit travel within China from Wuhan, while promoting international travel from that city and from its province, Hubei.

If reparations are sought, only those individuals and entities directly affected by the virus's spread should be compensated. A precedent must not be set for reparations to be determined by a disease's initial point of origin, for viruses do occur naturally and this process can only sometimes be controlled or mitigated. Instead, the demanding of compensation or the support of private lawsuits must be derivative of complex, preferably multinational, assessments of state malfeasance or criminality.

America's actions in this regard must not be framed in such a manner that may call into disputation the Public Debt Clause section of the Fourteenth Amendment, which states: "The validity of the public debt of the United States, authorized by law . . . shall not be questioned."[72] To do so would cause irreparable harm to the global financial system. It would also initiate reprisals by China that would destabilize world markets and economies. The dollar is the reserve currency for the world; it is the vehicle for international trade. Therefore, America's resolve to honor its debts can never be placed in question.

ACTIONS:

- Entrench principles and restrictions so China can buy no more of our corporations, universities, or national assets

- Strengthen CFIUS; create a new system for ranking nations, which will, in practice, exclude adversarial and belligerent states from amassing businesses or assets in our economy

- Prohibit, where possible, Huawei's planned deployment of their 5G networks

- Permit the pursuit of reparations or private lawsuits against the PRC, if evidence is accrued, only if such actions are consonant with U.S. national objectives and are derivative of state malfeasance or criminality

CHAPTER ELEVEN

FOUNDATION

Elaboration of new American measures to counteract China's coronavirus subterfuge, which is the most costly catastrophe in history aside from open warfare, should be structured to prevent a parallel event from occurring in the future. Key to such ability is the requirement for open, international inspections of biological laboratories in the same manner and with the same diligence as is required in the inspection of nuclear facilities.

A new, multinational initiative must integrate security and intelligence components to create a biological threat-response capability equivalent to that of our Nuclear Emergency Support Team (NEST), whose mission is to be "prepared to respond immediately to any type of radiological accident or incident anywhere in the world."[73] This task will be complex and extremely difficult because biological inspections will require foresight and a mastery over a far larger domain of possible agents than those involved in nuclear inspections and response capabilities. A multinational approach is indispensable, given the scope of this challenge.

Associated with this facility must be the creation of B Teams, of the type employed to assess Soviet strategic-force capabilities during the height of the Cold War. The function of such teams would be to provide a competitive and divergent view to that generated by a particular bureaucracy charged with making such assessments.[74] This friction, caused by competing appraisals, forces all investigators to hone their analyses, providing the decision-maker with a far more comprehensive and robust assessment of capabilities and threats than that which could be generated by a single source.

Just as we have created gradated codewords used by the government to classify nuclear accidents and events, the United States and its allies need to craft a common vocabulary for biological incidents. These designative terms should mirror those in use as nuclear-incident descriptors (Broken Arrow is the most commonly known term of this type: it refers to a nuclear-related event in which escalation is not at risk). The ordering and the use of these new terms within government will allow greatly enhanced and task-specific response times to biological emergencies.

These difficult initiatives must rest on an unprecedented diplomatic offensive. The United States must make common cause with its traditional allies to confront and to contain China. Further, developing nations must be included, for they have seen their assets appropriated by a communist state that foregoes no opportunity to exploit corrupt officials who sell out their own countries.

Importantly, Islamic nations must form a barrier opposed to Chinese expansionism because of both the PRC's rapaciousness and its doctrine. In addition, only an assembly of Islamic nations can press successfully for humane treatment for the twenty-five million Uyghur Muslims as well as other oppressed Muslim communities within China. The demand for a complete end to China's re-education camps must become a hallmark of American, allied, and Islamic efforts to end this atrocious abuse, which does not even leave the dead in peace, for it is the practice of the Communist Party of China to destroy Muslim cemeteries in Xinjiang, home to China's Uyghurs.

Australia has demonstrated resolve in its efforts to hold China to account. Its position astride crucial sea lines of communication is of immense military value. Therefore, the strategic Port of Darwin, which was leased for ninety-nine years in October 2015 by the Landbridge Group,[75] which is based in China, must come under total Australian control, with the existing lease terminated.

Enhanced relations with Indonesia, the world's fourth most populous country, must be pursued with vigor. Malaysia is also of great importance as are our traditional bilateral alliances with Japan and with the Republic of Korea.

Perhaps the most vital diplomatic action that may be taken would be the creation of a steadfast alliance between India and America. India's and China's respective populations are almost the same. India ranks third in the world in GDP (PPP) and will occupy at least this place for the foreseeable future. Fundamentally, America must move to a much closer relationship with India, which is democratic and is the product of many traditions, including its shared heritage with the United States of having once been part of the British Empire and thus enshrining both common customs and the English language.

Another component of this enhanced relationship could be greater coordination with the fifty-four-member-state Commonwealth of Nations. India became the first Commonwealth republic in 1950 on the day its constitution came into force. This association comprises 20 percent of the world's land and is a natural alternative for mutual development that may be substituted for China's BRI. Many avenues for growth are present in these relationships.

If not returned to the United States, any manufacturing now done in China, for or by American companies, can be better accomplished in India, for it is the world's largest democracy, and as such offers a degree of openness the PRC will never match. Military cooperation between the U.S. and China should largely cease (except for crisis de-escalation exercises); equivalent exchanges and exercises with India should be substituted.

In 2005, a "New Framework for the India-U.S. Defense Relationship" was signed by both nations.[76] This document and efforts in ensuing years to create a strategic partnership have received bipartisan support in the United States. It is time to augment this cooperation. In addition to joint military training, there is substantial space for military support and development.

What is not commonly known is India is one of only six countries in possession of nuclear-powered ballistic-missile submarines (SSBNs); India launched its first SSBN in 2009 and its second in 2017.[77] India also operates an aircraft carrier, which was originally built in 1987 for the Soviet Navy, and is completing its own indigenous design. The current plan by India to construct nuclear-powered attack submarines, advanced corvettes, and other vessels, is essential for regional defense.

The Obama Administration recognized the importance of India's pursuit of sea power. The "2015 Framework for the U.S.-India Defense"[78] committed both nations to collaboration regarding aircraft carriers and jet propulsion technology. This initiative built upon the 2009 sale of eight P-8I anti-submarine warfare aircraft to India, which marked an important advance in military commonality. Four more planes were later ordered and the purchase of an additional ten is contemplated. The 2017 Department of State approval of the sale of the MQ-9B armed drone,[79] which, as of 2020, has grown into a multibillion-dollar procurement of thirty unpiloted vehicles, to be split among India's armed forces, is indicative of future military initiatives we must prioritize. Though large, India's Navy requires modernization, with many ships in need of replacement. Enhanced navy-to-navy development, procurement, and operations should therefore be a vanguard to a much closer military relationship between the countries. Complicating this embrace is America's need to balance our relationship with Pakistan and to help ensure India's military capabilities support stability.

Pakistan was a member of both SEATO (the Southeast Asia Collective Defense Treaty) and CENTO (the Central Treaty Organization, which was comprised of Middle-Eastern states and the United Kingdom; America was foundational to the organization's creation, but never formalized its participation). Pakistan is also the recipient of renewed U.S. military assistance.

Through the creation of SEATO in 1954 and the Baghdad Pact (later known as CENTO) in 1955, the United States tried to recreate NATO in other areas to contain communist power. Both organizations were failures; SEATO was dissolved in 1977, CENTO, in 1979. The United States is party to a nonbinding security agreement with Australia and New Zealand, called the ANZUS Treaty. It has suffered severe internal disruptions and, unlike NATO, does not possess an integrated command structure nor designated forces from each country.

Consideration, therefore, should be given to conducting bilateral or multilateral talks to frame a new alliance structure, which could check the Communist Party of China's escalatory or revanchist actions. India, Australia, New Zealand,

Japan, the Republic of Korea, and America could form the core of a powerful defensive alliance. As with NATO, such an organization could, over time, expand its membership to include other states, such as Indonesia.

These developmental talks should be considered an outgrowth of the Quadrilateral Security Dialogue, which is held at the ministerial level between the United States, Australia, Japan, and India. These consultations were first initiated by Prime Minister Shinzo Abe of Japan in 2007.[80] They must now evolve into a more formal means of strategic and military cooperation for the noted states.

Two other militarily related initiatives must be pursued immediately. Freedom of navigation passages and exercises need to be accelerated through the waters China falsely claims as their own, with maximum U.S. naval power expressed; in this, we should include, when possible, ships of the British, the Australian, and the Japanese Navies.

To promote stability and deterrence, strong consideration should be given to the sale of F-35s to Taiwan due to the PRC's deployment of the advanced, fifth-generation Chengdu J-20 long-range fighter, which possesses some stealth characteristics. This transfer could follow the Department of State's recent approval for the sale of sixty-six F-16Vs to Taiwan;[81] alternatively, such a sale could serve as a substitute for some or all of these updated F-16s.

ACTIONS:

- **Create a threat response capability for biological events similar to our Nuclear Emergency Support Team (NEST)**
- **Establish B Teams to provide divergent views to that of the bureaucracy with regard to evolving threats and emergencies**

- Implement a series of codewords, for a range of biological events, to speed countermeasures
- Work with Islamic nations to stop China's systematic abuse of Chinese Muslims
- Enhance diplomatic and other efforts to stem the PRC's advance by coordinating closely with Australia, Japan, the Republic of Korea, Indonesia, and Malaysia
- Embrace India as part of a core American coalition; coordinate with India's military
- Seek to establish a new alliance structure to flank and to overmatch the PRC; work with India, Australia, New Zealand, Japan, and the Republic of Korea on this proposal
- Conduct augmented freedom of navigation transits in waters China wrongly claims
- Determine Taiwan's requirement for a fifth-generation fighter; consider the sale of F-35s to that island nation

CHAPTER TWELVE

ACTS

The Communist Party of China, in the wake of the coronavirus pandemic, has shown no signs of introspection or retrenchment. Its quest to dominate Hong Kong completely is in direct contravention of its prior commitments. China has broken the Sino-British Joint Declaration,[82] a treaty between itself and Britain, which designated Hong Kong to be a Special Administration Region of China, in which Hong Kong's capitalism and its freedoms, derived from British rule, could not be changed until 2047. This treaty was filed with the United Nations in 1985 after its ratification by the PRC and by Britain.

Elements within the PRC have considered claiming all of Mount Everest, though the mountain's summit lies astride Tibet's border with Nepal. More recently, China's media has argued for the future incorporation of Kyrgyzstan and Kazakhstan. Kyrgyz tribes were overwhelmed by the Qing dynasty in the eighteenth century. However, parts of Kyrgyzstan were ceded to Russia in the late nineteenth century, with the Russian Soviet Federative Socialist Republic obtaining full control in 1919.

The Dzungar Khanate, which fought the Kazakhs, was destroyed by soldiers of the Qing dynasty in the eighteenth century. Through this abhorrent campaign of annihilation, part of what is modern Kazakhstan was held by China's past dynastic empire. Following Russia's advances, the Bolsheviks' Red Army occupied Kazakhstan in 1920. Kyrgyzstan and Kazakhstan gained full sovereignty after the fall of the USSR: each declaring their independence from that empire in 1991. Afterward, Kazakhstan negotiated its present border, which is demarcated by a treaty with China. Kyrgyzstan also attained a border agreement with Beijing.

It is sobering to contemplate any element inside the PRC would propose annexing, through unspecified means, these two independent nations. Halting the PRC's encroachment and its attempted domination in Central Asia must be deemed critical to world security.

The problem is not the Chinese people, nor their proud heritage stretching back thousands of years; it is communism. We must, therefore, challenge Xi Jinping's governing principles as codified in "Xi Jinping Thought,"[83] for, in their effect, they substantiate one-man rule, which is inimical to individual initiative. Remarkably, they even appear untrue to the principles of Chinese communism and thus betray the country as just another despotic state.

Xi Jinping's duplicity and his malfeasance during this present pandemic have brought deserved international condemnation upon China and its communist rule. In so doing, Xi Jinping's actions are reminiscent of the dishonor Nikita Khrushchev caused the Soviet Union when he took his shoe in hand and banged it upon a table during the 902nd Plenary Meeting of the United Nations General Assembly in 1960.[84]

If powers in China remove Xi Jinping from office, this act alone would be insufficient to recalibrate relations to a point of normalcy; concrete remediation by the PRC must follow.

The Chinese threat must not be misrepresented, for our emphasis must be to disrupt the many caustic elements of China's geopolitical strategy. We must move to sanction the PRC. Had America done a tenth of what China has done to the world, even given the most charitable view of their acts, the PRC would do anything to make us pay.

If we are not willing to act and to act decisively, we are leaving the field and we are leaving it to an unhindered, unremorseful, and ravenous state with a degree of relative economic power we have not faced since the War of 1812. We dare not marginalize this crisis, for to do so is to admit defeat. This pandemic has almost certainly uncovered treachery by the PRC in its pursuit of world domination by whatever means necessary; the pandemic did not have to be planned, it is enough the communists seized on it, took advantage of it, and had special knowledge of its origin.

For deterrence to be established so a future malevolent actor is given notice of our capacities both to endure and to respond, America must exact a high price from the People's Republic of China for their patent deceitfulness and carnage. In this cause, we must seek the support of all the free nations of the world.

To be blocked, China must be denied access to intellectual property involving technology from corporate, governmental or educational entities, and be excluded from any degree of dominion over our media and our communications infrastructure. Tariffs need to be extended substantially if the PRC does not make all virus data and sites available to our scientists, so we may understand fully the genesis and the spread of the present pandemic. The PRC has to be made to release any COVID-19 whistleblowers and to eliminate all its wet markets, which, if left undisturbed, may incubate the next biological crisis.

An important step in confronting Chinese soft power is to limit its influence in the United Nations and its fifteen specialized agencies. President Trump's exit from the World Health Organization (WHO) is a necessary first step to stem this pillage.

In support of basic human rights, our government should contemplate holding a multinational symposium on the future of Tibet. Consideration should be given to the publication by the Department of State of a new counterpoint to *Tibet Transformed*, for this book, now decades old, was a centerpiece of Chinese propaganda fallaciously glorifying the advancement of the Tibetan people under Chinese rule. Thereafter, President Trump should meet with the Dalai Lama.

We are morally obligated to redouble our support for religious or other persecuted groups within China such as the Uyghurs and members of the Falun Gong. This should entail a broad interfaith dialog, which would also include Chinese and American Christian leaders, joined by Muslim clerics, Tibetan Buddhists, members of the Falun Gong, and other oppressed groups. Together, plans to avert religious or group persecution within China must be drawn and implemented.

ACTIONS:

- **Confront the PRC as to its abrogation of its treaty concerning Hong Kong; stand for freedom**
- **Deny the PRC's attempts to intimidate or to coerce the independent nations of Central Asia**
- **Explicate the errancies contained in "Xi Jinping Thought"**

- Explain Xi Jinping's malfeasance as manifested during the present crisis

- Enact steep tariffs if China does not allow the collection of important data concerning COVID-19; push China to release all COVID-19 whistleblowers and to close all wet markets

- Expose the lies China has promulgated concerning its occupation of Tibet

- Support religious liberty in China through an array of means; provide sustenance to oppressed groups, including the Falun Gong

CHAPTER THIRTEEN

CONDUITS

Retention of America's supremacy in the creation and in the application of soft power is fundamental, for hard power alone, given the world's interconnections and interdependence, is insufficient to channel future courses of events governing outcomes. China is on the verge, however, of becoming a peer competitor in its use of soft power and in its introduction of sharp power. This must not mean American stultification, but the burnishing of American advocacy and influence by vesting our power within the connectivity and informational domains we dominate. Such influence may only be retained if a floor of allied containment of China is realized.

The creation of a new, decentralized World Wide Web must be pursued with vigor. Censorship on major Web platforms threatens to limit personal freedom and expression. This very much supports the Communist Party of China's aims.

Brewster Kahle, computer engineer and founder of the Internet Archive, has joined Sir Tim Berners-Lee, the inventor of the World Wide Web, in calling for the creation of a decentralized Web, more resistant to government or corporate control. The creation of this new Web architecture would constitute a great advancement for freedom movements across the globe. Indeed, Kahle has stated, "China can make it impossible for people there to read things, and just a few big service providers are the de facto organizers of your experience. We have the ability to change all that."[85]

It may be argued that during the present pandemic, China's most abhorrent exports have been fear and disinformation. Yet these disgorgements were advanced by much of America's legacy media. Twice before this crisis and in the living memory of many Americans, our nation has experienced pandemics.

According to the CDC's website, during the 1957 Asian Flu, "The estimated number of deaths was 1.1 million worldwide and 116,000 in the United States."[86] The U.S. population in 1957 was 172 million; thus, adjusted for our present population, the Asian Flu would have killed 222,000 Americans. The Asian Flu pandemic did not change the economic life of America. While there was a recession from August 1957 to April 1958, the Asian Flu is not considered to be a primary causal factor.

Of the 1968 Hong Kong Flu, the CDC has written, "The estimated number of deaths was 1 million worldwide and about 100,000 in the United States."[87] America's population in 1968 was 201 million; adjusting for today, the Hong Kong Flu would have killed 164,000 Americans. A mild recession occurred from December 1969 through November 1970; neither it nor the pandemic affected America's economic condition.

While it may be contended the present pandemic had the potential to be much worse than the two preceding it, the present dread, stoked by a foreign power and by an echoic press, has certainly ruptured America's economy in ways inconceivable before this event. To cower, however, in the face of this pandemic and to not make the hard choices necessary to ensure American primacy is to be unfair to future generations.

How our country has thus far answered this pandemic is not repeatable: our present array of actions cannot be mounted if another wave or pandemic strikes. This is our gravest sin: we have shown China, Russia, and Iran, as well as terrorist actors, our nation may be disempowered if faced with a new pathogen. In so doing, we have done what no competent general would ever do, we have exposed our flank.

We must not afford the leadership of China the luxury of knowing what America will or will not do in response to this crisis. Our nation must explore a variety of tools and pressure points to counteract the Communist Party of China's intentions. As was done with the Soviet Union, we can no longer ignore the plight of captive nations held by China. To prosper, we must reclaim America's foundations and principles. We must reject utterly the adoption of a worldview that enshrines an all-powerful state serviced by great monopolies, for to accept this would be to grant China victory in a great, undeclared war.

ACTIONS:

- **Create a new, decentralized Web, supportive of cybersecurity, which will be able to penetrate the PRC's firewalls, to reach its citizenry**
- **Place the present pandemic in the context of past plagues our nation has overcome**

- Promote deterrence by exacting a high price for the PRC's unacceptable acts
- Answer the call of captive nations and peoples within China's empire

CHAPTER FOURTEEN

RESPONSIBILITIES

Vastly complicating the monumental tasks proposed herein is internal dissention within the United States unmatched since the Civil War. A national strategy must be enduring to be meaningful; it cannot be based on party rhetoric but must be rooted in an examination of our nation's founding principles. It has to survive changes in administrations until it is succeeded by a new national strategy, more relevant to some future time.

In 1943, Congressman Andrew May stated publicly, the Japanese Navy was setting its depth charges too shallowly. After the war, Admiral Charles Lockwood wrote that this admission prompted the Japanese to reconfigure their weapons: "ten submarines and 800 officers and men"[88] were lost as a result. Of equal gravity today are statements by political leaders that undermine the nation's power in a time of crisis. Only by returning to the principles of bipartisanship and the precept, "politics stops at the water's edge" may America be vested with its full abilities and its palisade of defense.

At the commissioning of the USS Henry M. Jackson (SSBN-730) in 1984, the bipartisan nature of Senator Jackson's extraordinary career was extolled, for it was marked by important agreements with members of both parties. Such independence of thought is almost impossible to imagine today but it is mandatory in the formulation, enactment, and entrenchment of a new national strategy, which may carry our nation forward.

Misconceptions by the press and by the public concerning the adversary we face are of equal concern. Any overarching strategy is doomed to failure if it is not supported by the public. Franklin Delano Roosevelt's fireside chats and Ronald Reagan's Oval Office addresses achieved the inclusion of the American public in crucial policy deliberations involving security. This president must use his own means to promote needed public dialog on the issues presented herein. President Trump must articulate the focus of the administration's policies and actions is directed at the Communist Party of China and not the Chinese people, who are the object of internal suppression.

The prime difference between the United States and the People's Republic of China must be explained clearly. Communists believe their citizens are part of a collective that exists to serve the state: this constitutes a hive mind. Free people are individuals. Indeed, America's Judeo-Christian heritage confirms God's relationship is with each person.

In the PRC, the state is sanctified. Our founding fathers believed this to be a cardinal mistake. They comprehended the great wisdom set out in Mark 12:17: "And Jesus answered and said to them, 'Render to Caesar the things that are Caesar's, and to God the things that are God's.' And they marveled at Him."

Jesus's statement in Mark is the first enunciation of the necessity for the separation of church and state. The paramount importance of which is best understood through the study of its contrapositive. If church and state are not separate, their natures and dominions are joined. This is not Christianity. This is not Judaism. It is unacceptable, for it posits, in effect, the divinity of the state.

If church and government are conjoined, such action is tantamount to a dictum that all the promises of religion are available in this world, but this is the antithesis of Jesus's teaching. Yet it is this antithesis that betrays the sleight of hand encountered in communism, for to erect heaven on earth, through man's labors, is an impossibility: the attempted inculcation of which has caused the death of hundreds of millions of lives, including tens of millions of men, women, and children in the People's Republic of China in the last century alone.

It is this substitution of what cannot be obtained—in place of God's promise of life after life—that has led China to become a force for evil in this world, for in China today, the state is sanctified. America must learn from this example and never attempt to enshrine an all-powerful state, for such a progression can only lead our nation into madness and despair.

In a democratic society, there is the capacity for self-examination and constraint. Competing forces and bases of power provide checks and balances to moderate extremism.

When political power combines with media and business establishments doing the government's bidding, and that government is unipolar, there can be no checks and balances and there will be no constraint. This is what we face in China today and what we could face in our country tomorrow: the existence of a single, all-powerful party, coupled with an echoic press, a technocracy, and a corporate, business class all in lockstep, eroding completely the preeminence of the individual.

The individual must always have primacy over the state. This principle is enshrined in our founding documents and it is enshrined in the Bible. This is because a government must be made up of individuals. A government must never be a fountainhead all to itself, for when it becomes such a thing, individual human beings are nothing; they are merely bricks to build the state, and the state is never completed.

Goethe, one of history's greatest geniuses, observed, "The hardest thing to see is what is in front of your eyes." This is the quandary of our time, for China has obscured its treachery as have statists in our midst, who have tempted their fellow citizens with promises of a utopia only available through God's eternal kingdom. Paradise can never be obtained through collectivism or through earthly means, as should be evident upon the most cursory study of the history of the PRC or any other communist nation.

If America does nothing else, the most basic action our nation must take is to expound the primacy of the individual above the state. It is this proclamation communists and totalitarians most fear. Its substantiation will be the basis for our meeting China on a high ground it can never successfully occupy.

ACTIONS:

- **Embrace our roots as a great nation**
- **Entrench bipartisanship, which must transcend political ambitions, for our nation to flourish**
- **Enshrine and propound "the Laws of Nature and of Nature's God" are our nation's unequaled armor against the expansionist imposition of communism and what that would foreshadow for the world**

EPILOGUE

THE HIGH GROUND

by Richard B. Levine

We must, as a nation, not fight change brought about by new technology but embrace it, for science and its progress cannot be halted. We must understand the friends we have. We must face our foes. We must plan for a future in which humans and computers are ever more connected and inseparable, though we must be diligent about maintaining the dominion of man over machine. We must use every advanced decision tool available to make far better decisions for our country. It is this technological progress that may be used and repurposed to check the power of established political and business elites.

In military strategy, nothing replaces occupying the high ground. Imagine our nation did not wage the Vietnam and the Iraq wars. Further imagine we did not spend $22 trillion on the failed war on poverty (introduced in 1964). Imagine a southern wall was completed decades ago and America let into our nation good people from all the corners of the world, but did so on the basis of a functioning immigration system seeking to attract the world's brightest and best.

Add to this, a different reality in which America funded the further development of the Saturn-class of rockets, including a nuclear-powered upper stage, which would have permitted a vastly expanded program of space exploration. Last, undo Congress's cancellation of the Superconducting Super Collider, which would have attracted many of the world's greatest scientists and engineers to our shores, and it is possible to envision an America that would have been wealthy today beyond measure, would have been supreme and uncontested militarily, and could have provided each of its citizens with futures of unlimited potential and wealth.

Very few decisions need to be changed for a nation's history either to be impoverished or be unsurpassed. Many times during the past sixty years, America chose the wrong path: we now are paying the price.

President Trump has endeavored ardently to reclaim America's glory. His defeat or his reelection in the coming election will constitute the most profound turning point in American history since at least the presidency of Abraham Lincoln.

NOTES

1. See https://plato.stanford.edu/entries/reflective-equilibrium/
2. See https://www.foxnews.com/politics/jv-terrorists-obama-under-fire-for-having-underestimated-militant-threat-in-iraq-syria
3. See https://www.forbes.com/sites/lorenthompson/2011/12/19/how-to-waste-100-billion-weapons-that-didnt-work-out/#79b44b6d-1cb5
4. See https://www.pressherald.com/2019/10/10/navys-new-7-8-billion-zumwalt-destroyer-is-now-running-6-years-late/; https://physicstoday.scitation.org/do/10.1063/PT.4.1205/full/ (Note: Although the Navy proposed a reduction in the procurement of Zumwalt-class destroyers in 2008, due to budgetary pressures brought about by the wars in Afghanistan and Iraq, construction of the class was underway and could have been extended. The program, however, was reduced permanently to three ships in April 2009 in the Department of Defense's proposed 2010 budget.)
5. See https://www.boeing.com/defense/f-15ex/
6. See https://www.defense-aerospace.com/articles-view/release/3/211721/us-air-force-begins-b_52-re_engining-program.html
7. See https://www.forbes.com/sites/lorenthompson/2019/11/08/ten-things-we-know-for-sure-about-the-air-forces-secret-b-21-bomber/#760583921caf
8. See https://www.lockheedmartin.com/en-us/products/f-35/f-35-capabilities.html

9. See https://www.military.com/equipment/gerald-r-ford-class-aircraft-carrier
10. See https://futurefrigate.com/specifications/
11. See https://www.airforce-technology.com/projects/abl/
12. See https://www.beltandroad.news/2019/05/02/world-bank-gives-credit-to-belt-road-construction-2/
13. See https://www.dailymail.co.uk/news/article-3485465/amp/VP-Biden-meets-Jordans-King-Abdullah-key-Mideast-ally.html
14. See https://www.christianpost.com/news/state-john-kerry-isis-atro cities-christians-genocide-islamic-daesh.html
15. See https://nymag.com/intelligencer/2016/03/john-kerry-says-isis-is-committing-genocide.html
16. See https://www.breitbart.com/2020-election/2020/01/14/fact-check-joe-biden-falsely-claims-to-have-defeated-isis/
17. See https://www.whitehouse.gov/presidential-actions/presidential-memorandum-plan-defeat-islamic-state-iraq-syria/
18. See https://www.aljazeera.com/news/2019/03/hundreds-isil-fight ers-surrender-syria-baghouz-sdf-190306160315079.html; https://www.thesun.co.uk/news/8622375/isis-jihadis-surrender-syri an-forces-baghouz/
19. See https://www.npr.org/2019/10/27/773791704/u-s-targets-isis-locations-in-syria-attack
20. See https://time.com/5711809/al-baghdadi-islamic-state-isis-dead/
21. See https://www.defensenews.com/smr/nato-2020-defined/2020/01/08/trump-wants-nato-to-be-more-involved-in-the-middle-east-that-may-take-some-convincing/
22. See https://www.fairobserver.com/region/middle_east_north_africa/saudi-arabia-counterterrorism-alliance-arab-world-news-head lines-97121/
23. See https://www.theguardian.com/world/2018/may/08/iran-deal-trump-withdraw-us-latest-news-nuclear-agreement
24. See http://www.medwelljournals.com/abstract/?doi=sscience.2016.12 77.1282
25. See https://www.pbs.org/wgbh/pages/frontline/tehranbureau/2010/10/iran-primer-irans-nuclear-program.html
26. See https://www.bloomberg.com/news/articles/2018-12-05/huawei-cfo-arrested-in-canada-as-u-s-seeks-her-extradition
27. See https://crsreports.congress.gov/product/pdf/R/R45898
28. See https://www.reuters.com/article/us-china-djibouti-idUSKB-N1AH3E3
29. See https://journal-neo.org/2014/04/15/rus-vtoroe-dy-hanie-ki tajskoj-strategii-nit-zhemchuga-chast-1/

30. See https://www.reuters.com/article/us-iran-nuclear-turkey-idUSK BN1KT210
31. See https://news.trust.org/item/20180715081915-033tg/
32. See https://www.yenisafak.com/en/world/what-if-a-muslim-army-was -established-against-israel-2890448
33. See https://www.defense.gov/Explore/News/Article/Article/841966/ obama-briefed-on-turkey-situation-incirlik-closed-but-safe- officials-say/
34. See https://www.theatlantic.com/news/archive/2017/06/chinese-no bel-laureate-released-from-prison/531738/
35. See https://www.worldfoodprize.org/en/dr_norman_e_borlaug/exten ded_biography/
36. See https://www.nytimes.com/1999/05/11/world/clinton-approves -technology-transfer-to-china.html; https://www.salon.com/1998/ 05/29/newsa_3/
37. See http://www.ggdc.net/Maddison/China_book/Chapter_2.pdf
38. See https://obamawhitehouse.archives.gov/the-press-office/2015/ 09/25/fact-sheet-us-china-economic-relations
39. Ibid.
40. Ibid.
41. See https://www.pbs.org/wgbh/pages/frontline/shows/plague/sverd lovsk/
42. See https://www.congress.gov/bill/116th-congress/senate-bill/945? overview=closed
43. See https://www.indiewire.com/2019/07/tom-cruises-jacket-taiwanese -japanese-patches-in-top-gun-maverick-trailer-1202160078/#!
44. See https://www.cruz.senate.gov/?p=press_release&id=5083
45. See https://www.dailymail.co.uk/news/article-2428051/Hitlers-reign -terror--Film-warning-dangers-Nazi-Germany-US-railroad-heir- 75-years.html (Note: Cornelius Vanderbilt IV was known throughout his life as Cornelius Vanderbilt Jr.)
46. See http://www.tcm.com/this-month/article.html?id=79866%7C313
47. See https://www.dailymail.co.uk/news/article-5006235/Hitler-s-West -Coast-takeover-foiled-Jewish-lawyer.html; https://www.goodreads. com/book/show/33590281-hitler-in-los-angeles
48. See https://www.webfx.com/blog/internet/the-6-companies-that- own-almost-all-media-infographic/ (Note: Because of the large number of businesses noted, ownership of a particular company may be subject to change; therefore, this infographic may not represent actual corporate ownership at the present or at a future point in time for all the companies represented.)

49. See https://www.washingtonpost.com/opinions/2020/04/14/state
-department-cables-warned-safety-issues-wuhan-lab-study
ing-bat-coronaviruses/
50. See https://www.thestar.com.my/opinion/letters/2019/05/13/sustain
ability-is-key-to-successful-bri/
51. See https://qz.com/africa/1560998/djibouti-dp-world-port-case-
challenges-chinas-belt-and-road/
52. See https://www.cbsnews.com/news/rosneft-russian-oil-could-claim
-us-oil-trump-cfius/; https://home.treasury.gov/news/press-releases/
sm594;https://www.washingtonpost.com/world/2019/01/29/how-cit
go-us-oil-company-became-venezuelas-lifeline/ (Note: The United
States Government in January 2019 sanctioned PDVSA, the government of Venezuela's oil and natural gas company, which had acquired
ownership of Citgo in 1986 and 1990; following these sanctions, Citgo, a United States-based company, severed ties with PDVSA.)
53. See https://www.nytimes.com/2020/05/18/business/china-loans-co
ronavirus-belt-road.html
54. See https://www.cgdev.org/blog/debt-crisis-looming-researchers
-who-estimated-chinas-hidden-lending-respond-their-critics
55. See https://thecommonwealth.org/member-countries
56. See https://www.historytoday.com/archive/months-past/visigoths-
sack-rome
57. See https://www.world-nuclear.org/information-library/country-pro
files/countries-a-f/china-nuclear-power.aspx
58. See https://carnegieendowment.org/2018/05/14/future-of-nuclear
-power-in-china-introduction-pub-76312
59. See https://www.businessinsider.com/10-biggest-cities-22nd-century
-2016-2#2-kinshasa-democratic-republic-of-the-congo-835-mil-
lion-people-9
60. See https://www.ucpress.edu/book/9780520301337/national-power
-and-the-structure-of-foreign-trade
61. See https://www.justice.gov/opa/pr/court-imposes-maximum-fine-
sinovel-wind-group-theft-trade-secrets
62. See https://defensesystems.com/articles/2011/11/08/sasc-hearing-
counterfeit-parts-dod-supply-chain.aspx
63. See http://www.ipcommission.org/report/IP_Commission_Report
_052213.pdf
64. See https://archives.caltech.edu/news/tsien.html (Note: The scientist's name has also been given as Hsue-Shen Tsien and, later, as
Qian Xuesen.)
65. See https://fas.org/sgp/crs/misc/IF10667.pdf
66. See http://www.nbcnews.com/id/7695811/ns/business-world_busi-
ness/t/chinas-lenovo-acquires-ibm-division/#.XycH9ChKiUk;

https://www.cnet.com/news/lenovo-closes-acquisition-of-motorola
-mobility-from-google/
67. See https://www.foxbusiness.com/money/china-buys-smithfield-
foods-owned-wh-group; https://www.pbs.org/newshour/show/whos
-behind-chinese-takeover-worlds-biggest-pork-producer
68. See https://screenrant.com/legendary-pictures-china-wanda-group
-purchase/; https://www.latimes.com/entertainment/envelope/co
town/la-et-ct-wanda-buys-legendary-entertainment-20160111-
story.html
69. See https://www.latimes.com/entertainment-arts/business/story/
2020-07-28/amc-and-universal-reach-landmark-deal-for-early-
home-releases; https://www.reuters.com/article/us-dalianwanda-
amc-exclusive-idUSKCN1LL2DZ
70. See https://www.treasury.gov/press-center/press-releases/Pages/jl0679
.aspx; https://digitalcommons.law.uga.edu/cgi/viewcontent.cgi?article
=1528&context=gjicl
71. See https://home.treasury.gov/news/press-releases/sm457
72. See https://constitution.congress.gov/constitution/amendment-14/
73. See https://web.archive.org/web/20060923060954/http://www.nv
.doe.gov/library/factsheets/NEST.pdf
74. See https://www.commentarymagazine.com/articles/richard-pipes-2/
team-b-the-reality-behind-the-myth/
75. See https://www.theguardian.com/australia-news/2015/oct/13/chin
ese-company-secures-99-year-lease-of-darwin-port-in-506m-deal;
https://www.abc.net.au/news/2015-10-13/chinese-company-land-
bridge-wins-99-year-darwin-port-lease/6850870
76. See https://dod.defense.gov/Portals/1/Documents/pubs/US-IND-
Fact-Sheet.pdf
77. See https://www.navyrecognition.com/index.php/news/defence-
news/2017/10136-december-2017-naval-defense-news/5822-in-
dia-launched-its-second-arihant-class-ssbn-ballistic-missile-sub-
marine-arighat.html
78. See https://archive.defense.gov/pubs/2015-Defense-Framework.pdf
79. See https://www.defensenews.com/breaking-news/2017/06/23/mq
-9b-drone-sale-for-india-to-be-ok-d/
80. See https://usiofindia.org/publication/usi-journal/prospects-for-the
-quad-in-the-indo-pacific/
81. See https://www.janes.com/defence-news/news-detail/taiwanese
-f-16v-procurement-activated-with-engine-contract
82. See https://www.theguardian.com/politics/2020/jul/01/china-is-
breaking-hong-kong-treaty-with-uk-says-boris-johnson
83. See https://thediplomat.com/2020/07/how-will-the-eu-answer-
chinas-turn-toward-xi-jinping-thought-on-diplomacy/;https://www

.whitehouse.gov/briefings-statements/chinese-communist-par
tys-ideology-global-ambitions/
84. See https://enacademic.com/dic.nsf/enwiki/9697109
85. See https://www.livemint.com/Consumer/CIT2ltKmxDtK9EtUR
4lPMJ/The-webs-creator-looks-to-reinvent-it.html
86. See https://www.cdc.gov/flu/pandemic-resources/1957-1958-pan
demic.html
87. See https://www.cdc.gov/flu/pandemic-resources/1968-pandemic
.html (Note: U.S. death tolls due to COVID-19 are likely inflated
due to numbers not distinguishing between persons who died from
the virus as opposed to persons who died *with* the virus.)
88. See http://www.ww2pacific.com/congmay.html